**Living in the path of Totality**

# We Survived the Eclipse!

Accounts of the 2017 Total Solar Eclipse in Franklin, NC and Surrounding Areas

*Claire Suminski*

Edited by: Claire Suminski

Copyright 2018 by Claire Suminski

All rights reserved.

No part of this book may be used or reproduced in any manner whatsoever without written permission.
Contact Suminski Family Books, 32 Jim Berry Road, Franklin, NC 28734

First Edition
ISBN 978-0-9985899-8-5

Library of Congress Control Number (LCCN): 2017961613

Published by Red Press Co.

Redpressco.com

# Table of Contents

Forward by Doug Woodward

<u>Introduction Section</u>

      Introduction by Claire Suminski .......1

      Be Prepared: Macon County News .......2

      Tourism Groups Prepare: Smoky Mountain News .......3

      Atmospheric Impact and Questions .......5

      Flashbacks to Past Eclipses: Art Poling: Alaska 1963 .......6

                         Ron Cabe: Hawaii 1991 .......7

      Moon Pies .......9

<u>Part One: Franklin Gatherings</u>

      Downtown Franklin .......13

      Otto Observatory .......18

      Franklin Chamber of Commerce .......20

      Macon County Library .......22

      Entegra Bank .......25

      Forest Service District Report .......28

      Cowee School, Arts and Heritage Center .......31

      The Franklin Press .......32

<u>Part Two: Smaller Gatherings in the Franklin Area</u>

      Carringer Farms .......34

      Irene Tinsdale .......35

      John & Cathryn Sill .......36

      Sybil Potts Cabe Major .......38

      Suminski Farmette .......40

      Dorothy Deal & Opal Brown .......43

      Elliot Family .......44

      Susan Ervin & Bill McLarney .......45

      Winding Stair Nursery .......46

Part Three: Gatherings West of Franklin

    Town of Andrews …….49

    Andrews Airport …….52

    Andrews Middle School …….55

    Edie Thorpe …….58

Part Four: Gatherings East of Franklin

    Western Carolina University …….62

    Mary Jo (Hooper) Cobb …….65

    Cowee Bald Tower: Ken Johnson …….66

    Kyle & Maggie Jennings …….68

Eclipse Extras

    Original Song by Rachel Stewart "We Survived the Night of Day"

    Games, Puzzles, & Poems

    Eric Haggert Biography

    Acknowledgements

    Editor & Graphic Designer Information

    Game and Puzzle Answer Key

# Foreword
## By: Doug Woodward

When the Great Solar Eclipse of August 2017, sliced its way across the United States from Oregon to South Carolina, it brought together entire communities, as well as strangers, in comradery that is rarely experienced in these times. Where were you on that afternoon? Whether you were in the path of totality or somewhere in the wings, it is likely that you will remember the dimming of that day for the rest of your life.

That is certainly true for our family and the friends who joined us here at our home near Franklin, North Carolina. In the summertime, our pond is a favorite spot for swimming and picnicking and, we felt, would be a perfect venue for eclipse watching. My wife, Trish, checked it out the day before and sure enough, in mid-afternoon, the sun would be visible from any part of the pond. We splashed into the water on innertubes and floats, keeping our eclipse glasses dry. As totality enveloped us, the celestial sight was indeed awe-inspiring, but the changes taking place around us were surreal – the eerie quiet, the strange shadows, fleeting flashes of light appearing unexpectedly. Yes, we will remember.

And so many others have similar – yet unique – experiences of that day. Those of us who live in Macon County were gifted with the path of totality without having to make a pilgrimage to be part of it. Claire Suminski, the author of this book, together with her family, sought out friends throughout our community, to record and share their own impressions of that memorable event.

When it comes to knowledge of our community, the folks that comprise it, and the ability to elicit stories from friends, few individuals could do the task better than Claire. For the thirty years that we have known Claire and her husband Joe, we have seen them give their time and energy to worthwhile projects that we all benefit from, while at the same time nurturing four children to adulthood with values similar to their own. And, I should mention, that they not only give to the community, they are leaders of it.

Many of you have been thrilled to read the Suminski Family's series of Cowee Sam children's books, which give you a glimpse of their family life and the adventures of one of their most beloved family members, their loyal Great Pyrenees, Cowee Sam. Now they have collected a memorable series of adventures from friends who experienced the Great Solar Eclipse of 2017. Enjoy!

Doug Woodward, author of
Wherever Waters Flow, A Lifelong Love Affair with Wild Rivers
You Took the Kids Where? Adventuring While Your Children are Young

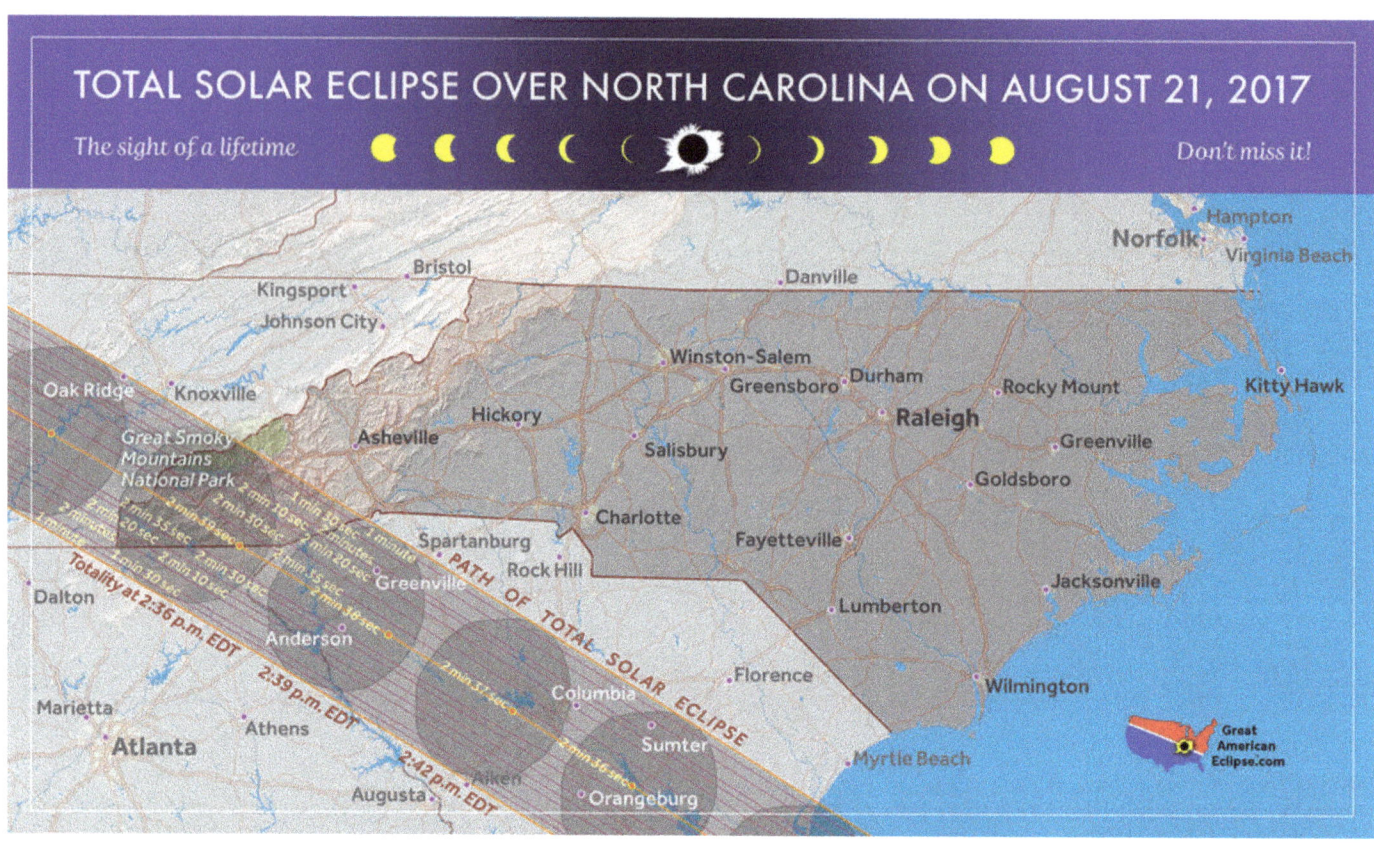

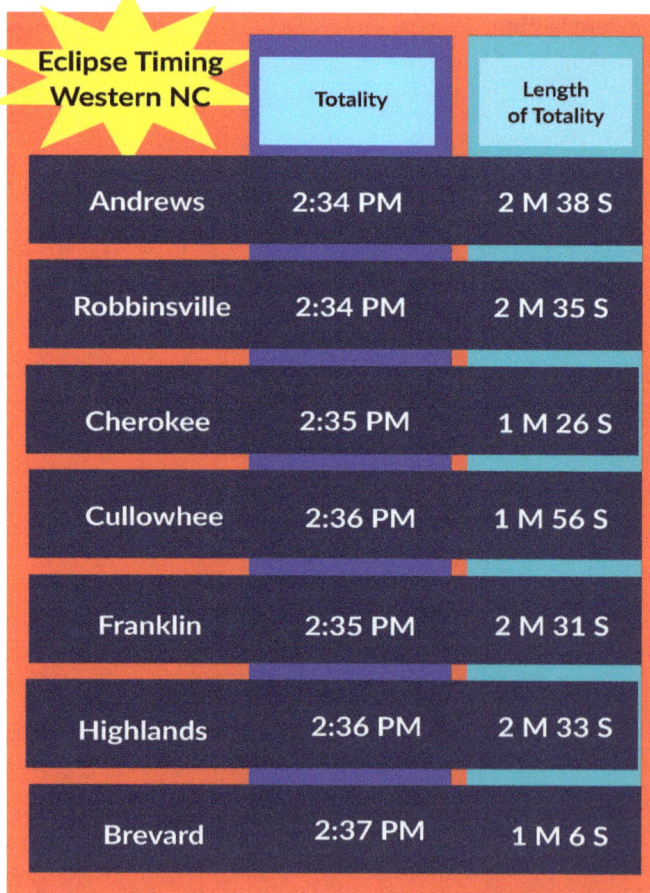

| Eclipse Timing Western NC | Totality | Length of Totality |
|---|---|---|
| Andrews | 2:34 PM | 2 M 38 S |
| Robbinsville | 2:34 PM | 2 M 35 S |
| Cherokee | 2:35 PM | 1 M 26 S |
| Cullowhee | 2:36 PM | 1 M 56 S |
| Franklin | 2:35 PM | 2 M 31 S |
| Highlands | 2:36 PM | 2 M 33 S |
| Brevard | 2:37 PM | 1 M 6 S |

## Introduction:

### This is our story.

It has been an adventure collecting the accounts and pictures in this book. Several times during the writing process, I was reminded of another occurrence in nature, that I experienced as a young woman, for which there was no advance preparation or warning. The morning of May 18, 1980, my husband and I were enjoying a motorcycle ride in the countryside West of Clarkston, Washington. As noon approached the whole dome of sky took on a peculiar greenish grey color, and it became eerily quiet. Had we been invaded? Had a bomb gone off somewhere? We did not have a cell phone. No radio. No Facebook to consult, no one to tweet, not a person in sight to ask. We knew that we needed to find out what was happening and made a bee line for the burger joint on the edge of town. Joe asked the window attendant at the drive-in window what was going on. He replied, "It's all over the radio, Mount St. Helens blew!"

We were 347 miles away from the eruption, but the ash reached the twin cities of Clarkston, Washington, and Lewiston, Idaho shortly after noon, and it fell for months. Although there were rumblings far in advance of this catastrophe, there was no way of pinpointing exactly if and when it would happen. Early that morning a 5.1 earthquake triggered a landslide that unleashed a volcanic eruption which lasted for hours, resulting in the death of 57 people and the loss of over 250 homes. The day Mount St. Helens blew, many were caught off guard.

Throughout history, there have been partial and total eclipses that have come upon mankind without warning. What must our predecessors have thought when the sun disappeared in the middle of the day? Did they wonder if the sun would come back?

On Monday, August 21, 2017, we enjoyed the thrill of a total eclipse of the sun. Its path stretched from West coast to East, and was called, "The Great American Eclipse." In this age of communication, we knew about it far in advance and were prepared. That afternoon Macon County, North Carolina was in the Path of Totality and at 2:36 pm, the moon passed in front of the sun for an amazing 2 minutes and 30 seconds. As totality struck Franklin, I was reminded that only God, who made the sun, moon, and stars, in all of His magnificence, could arrange for this celestial happening. The bugs, birds, and animals may have been surprised, but in the year 2017, in America, a person would practically have to be living under a rock not to know this was happening. For Western North Carolinians, it was a once in a lifetime experience. Most enjoyed a clear view of the eclipse that day, but for many, their view was partially obscured by passing clouds, and for a few, dark clouds or even rain prevented them from seeing anything at all. But it happened, right on schedule. Citizen or visitor, male or female, young or old: we were here for the Great American Eclipse. This is our story.

Claire Suminski - September 11, 2017

## In Anticipation of the Unknown, We were Advised........

Suggestions for navigating the eclipse:

– Be prepared for crowds, lines and traffic. Areas around construction zones in east Franklin and intersections in downtown Highlands are expected to be especially congested. Allow extra time for travel.
– Have snacks, water and first-aid supplies on hand in case crowds/lines/traffic becomes significant while you are traveling.
– Be aware of the hazards of the area especially this time of year including steep and winding rural roads, heavy and slow moving traffic, severe thunderstorms, and trip and fall hazards particularly around waterfalls and other trail areas.
– Have an emergency kit and emergency plan; make sure family members or friends know your schedule, when you are expected to return, and your plan if something happens.

Suggestions for businesses and employers:

– Prepare for a larger than normal influx of customers. Goods should be ordered and staffing adjusted accordingly.
– Be aware that some visitors unfamiliar with the area may be in authorized and unauthorized areas.
– Encourage your employees to be prepared with full fuel tanks and other necessary supplies to avoid long lines and other delays that could occur should the influx of visitors be significant.
– Talk to suppliers, particularly those out of the local area, that may not anticipate the event. Some deliveries might need to be adjusted accordingly.
With little information available except estimates for potential visitors and no event in recent history comparable on which to base any estimates, Macon County Emergency Management recommends treating this event as a significant travel holiday event and will continue to monitor the event as it draws near providing information as it becomes available and update plans as necessary.
Important information such as viewing safety can be found at http://eclipse2017.nasa.gov

Reprinted with permission:   Macon County News August 2, 2017

**Smoky Mountain news**

reprinted condensed version by permission of
Smoky Mountain News

# Tourism groups prepare for rare eclipse in 2017

Smokey Mountain News
Tourism groups prepare for rare eclipse in 2017
Written by Jessi Stone    June 22, 2016

Jackson County will be one of the best places in the entire nation to witness the rare celestial event when the moon passes directly between the sun and the Earth.

According to maps from NASA, Jackson and Macon counties are in the direct path of totality, which means certain areas in the Western North Carolina region will be in complete darkness during the eclipse. Nick Breedlove has Jackson County broken down to a science. "In Sylva, we will have 1 minute, 45 seconds of complete totality; Cullowhee: 1 minute, 55 seconds; Cashiers 2 minutes, 23 seconds," he said. "The partial eclipse will begin at 1:06 p.m. in Sylva and the total eclipse will take place at 2:35 p.m."

As the director of tourism development for the county, Breedlove knows these details will be essential in making sure Jackson County is prepared for the masses of people expected to descend upon the area. Not only will the eclipse be an exciting experience for many residents, but it could be a huge economic boon for the tourism industry.

"The event has the potential to draw crowds from all over the Southeast to our corner of North Carolina," Breedlove said. "It's hard to estimate the number of people that will come for the event, but between residents and tourists from outside of the county traveling to see it, there's potential for a massive influx of individuals who will travel to witness the once-in-a-lifetime event."

Early planning

Breedlove first heard about the eclipse in February from tourism colleague and Western Carolina University hospitality professor Steve Morse. It's been a major topic of conversation at every tourism conference they've attended this year.

Franklin resident David Hubbs brought the issue before the Franklin Board of Aldermen a couple of months ago in hopes the town would begin marketing the eclipse early.

"On Monday, Aug. 21, 2017, the moon will pass between the Earth and the sun and the moon will obscure the sun," Hubbs told the board. "We will have a total solar eclipse for over two minutes. I think the town should take advantage of this event — it's not too early to promote Franklin as a viewing destination, and I think we could fill every hotel and restaurant for two to four days in advance of this event."

Safety factors

Over the last couple of months, Breedlove has been working to organize a stakeholders meeting to discuss the logistics and marketing strategy for such a major undertaking. About 30 of those stakeholders, including SCC, Jackson County Schools, Emergency Management and Public Safety county staff, astronomy professors and airport officials, met at Southwestern Community College to begin hashing out the details.

"The event will take a significant amount of planning and education to ensure people experience it safely and enjoy it to its fullest potential," Breedlove said. "I've been talking with other eclipse planning directors from across the country and sharing ideas back and forth about how we can best plan for this unique experience."

In his research on eclipses, Breedlove has discovered other factors that could present safety issues other than a massive onslaught of people. Drivers on the road during the event could cause safety issues. Animals tend to notice the changes associated with any big celestial event and may retreat to their crates, make excessive noise or run away. "Many things will happen all at the same time," Breedlove said.

Weather is the one thing that is impossible to predict and control as WNC prepares to host thousands of people for the eclipse. An overcast or rainy day could put a major damper on viewing the eclipse. With some of the highest elevations in the eclipse track, WNC could luck out with a gorgeous clear day. On the other hand, the mountains can quickly become notoriously cloudy. "Historically we've had good weather over the last ten years in Sylva on Aug. 21, so we're hoping for a repeat next year," Breedlove said.

Right place at the right time

The eclipse path of totality (total darkness) is narrow — about 70 miles wide — with Balsam bordering the west end of the path and Cleveland, Georgia, bordering the east end of the path. The path runs northwest up through Kansas City, Missouri and parts of Oregon.

It will be the first time in 26 years the United States has experienced a total solar eclipse. There have been several others in the last few years, but they've only been visible in Europe, Asia, Australia and Africa. "Totalities happen all the time across the world, but they don't always occur over land since 75 percent of the Earth is water; the shadows often fall across the ocean making it inaccessible," Breedlove said. "For many locations in America, it's been 300 to 400 years since the last totality. In Atlanta the last one was in 1778 and the next one won't be until 2078. It is in our best interest regionally to work together and share ideas with one another," he said. "A high tide raises all boats, so I'd love to collaborate to see how we can market this event to draw people to the region for the event."

*It will be the first time in 26 years the United States has experienced a total solar eclipse.*

# Atmosheric Impact of the Solar Eclipse

The ionosphere is a large section of the earth's atmosphere. Parts of the ionosphere are highly charged. Solar radiation hitting the ionosphere ionizes (conversion of atoms and molecules into ion or ions by removing one or more electrons) and develops a layer called plasma. During an eclipse, when the moon blocks some of the solar radiation from reaching the Earth, there are big changes in the electrical conductivity of the ionosphere. These changes ripple out, affecting Earth's own electric and magnetic fields. Scientists gathered around the United States to study these effects because eclipse-related disturbances may affect not only the atmosphere, but the entire geomagnetic field, which can put satellites, astronauts, and more at risk.

## Questions you may ask:

**COULD THIS BE WHY THERE HAVE BEEN SO MANY HURRICANES WEEKS AFTER THE TOTAL SOLAR ECLIPSE?**
According to the Newsweek article, written on September 26th, 2017, "No, the Solar Eclipse did not cause all these hurricanes". Here is a link to that article:
http://www.newsweek.com/total-solar-eclipse-cause-hurricane-harvey-irma-maria-669783

**IS THIS WHY SOME PEOPLE WORE ALUMINUM FOIL HATS DURING THE ECLIPSE?**
Yes, although there have been studies to show that these changes have no effect on the human brain. We here at Suminski Family Books think that most people wearing these hats were just having fun with the idea of radiation affecting them and did not really believe that it did.

# Flashback to July 20, 1963

Painting courtesy of : Marilyn Miller

Some of our eclipse-watchers have traveled to other points far and near to view previous total eclipses of the sun.

Art Poling, who drove into Franklin from the Raleigh area, traveled to Canada as a boy to view the total solar eclipse which occurred on July 20, 1963. The path of totality of that eclipse passed over Japan and Russia and was only visible in North America in Alaska, Canada, and Maine. Art's father worked in the field of science and knew that this would be a significant event for his family to witness.

This is what Art had to say, "The total eclipse I saw with my parents was in July, 1963 when we were on vacation in Canada. Dad put together our solar viewing tool, which consisted of exposed photographic film. During the time in Franklin, we saw a similar pattern to what I remember seeing in 1963. As things began to get darker, the temperature dropped, various animals quieted down and the crickets started chirping." The 1963 eclipse was covered in a Peanuts comic strip that summer, with Linus demonstrating safe eclipse viewing options for that time period. Now we can go online and easily order certified safe, solar eclipse viewing glasses, as long as the manufacturers don't run out! We have come a long way with safe eclipse viewing, but God supplies the eclipses and THAT has not changed.

# Flashback to July 11, 1991

This was not Ron Cabe's first total eclipse of the sun. Ron was the Project Manager for a construction crew in Hawaii on the island of Maui. His crew was building a golf course on the top of a mountain for Japanese investors. From the project area, he had a great view of the ocean and of "The Happy Cow Farm". July 11, 1991, as Ron looked out on the sea, he could see the darkened sky from the total eclipse of the sun, racing across the water at a very high speed. As it approached the island and began to cover the sun, the sky started to grow dark, and he could see the Happy Cows below heading for their barns. Visitors had paid a lot of money to come to Hawaii and watch this eclipse from the comfortable beaches and hotels below. The lower elevation ended up with a cloud covered view, and the tourists could not see it. However, Ron and his crew and the Happy Cows had a bird's eye view. It was a thrilling experience for him, and he did not have to leave work to see it!

*It was a thrilling experience for him, and he did not have to leave work to see it!*

Quote from the Great American Eclipse Website:
The total solar eclipse of July 11, 1991, was the last to touch any of the 50 United States. Many flew to Hawaii for this eclipse, and sadly most were disappointed by unseasonably cloudy weather on the Kona coast of the Big Island. Many others flew or drove to the tip of Baja California and were rewarded with excellent views of an extremely long duration eclipse, up to 6 minutes and 53 seconds.

# Moon Pies sales soar, during their 100th year, as people celebrate the Total Solar Eclipse!

For the Moon Pie Corporation, headquartered in Nashville, Tennessee, 2017 was a banner year. Their 100th Anniversary was the same year as the Great American Solar Eclipse!

Many Solar Eclipse enthusiasts, planning refreshments for their viewing parties, included Moon Pies on their menus. Tory Johnston, Head of Marketing for the Moon Pie Corporation said that sales during 4 weeks before and 4 weeks after the eclipse rose by over 20%. It was easily the best 2 month period for moon pie sales in more than a decade! Sales of Moon Pie Originals, Minis, and Doubles all rose.

The Moon Pie Corporation made a big social media push, promoting Moon Pies as the perfect Solar Eclipse party snack. Southern Living, People Magazine, and others picked up on this idea. It went viral!

So many people rushed to local retail outlets to buy Moon Pies, that soon their customer service department was buried under re-orders. Regular customers like Walmart and Publix were sold out and their shelves were empty. Things are back to normal now. But 2017 will always be remembered by the Moon Pie Corporation as a year that will go down in Moon Pie History.

# Unusual Eclipse Occurrences

**Tumbling Temperatures**

**Anxious Animals**

**Shady Shadows**

**Captivating Corona**

**Prominent Planets**

*Did you see anything unusual?*

# Part One:
# Franklin Gatherings

"To look out at this kind of creation out here and not believe in God is to me impossible."

### John Glenn
— On his second space flight on space shuttle Discovery in 1998.

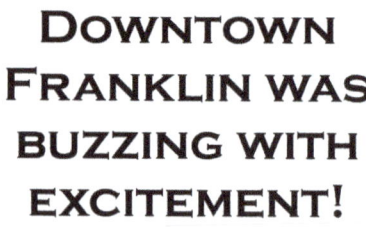

# Downtown Franklin was buzzing with excitement!

These beautiful photographs were taken by Katie Farris.

# Franklin Hosts Thousands on Main Street

Tens of thousands of people flocked into Macon County over the weekend to experience the Great American Eclipse. While experts and algorithms predicted an influx of visitors anywhere from 10,000 to 100,000, the truth lay somewhere in the middle, with one certainty standing true, the solar eclipse was truly an unforgettable experience.

Town officials estimated that 10,000 people descended on Main Street for the town-sponsored Eclipse Block Party. The town gave away a steady stream of eclipse glasses, with some still available by the time the eclipse started. Inflatables filled Iotla Street, and the Lazy Hiker Brewing Company set up a beer garden and yard games on the north end of the street.

- The Macon County News
August 23, 2017

*The Solar Eclipse was truly an unforgettable experience.*

Downtown Franklin was packed with visitors on the day of the eclipse. The town staff ordered and gave out over 2,000 pair of glasses.
They estimate that about 10,000 guests were there to view the eclipse. Guests came from as far away as California, New Hampshire, Maine, New York, Virginia, Florida, and even Russia and Venezuela!

Mayor, Bob Scott, was a strong presence that day, greeting guests and taking pictures, which are featured on this page. He said it was so memorable to spend this historic occasion with several thousand new friends!

Summer Woodard, who has served as the Franklin Town Manager for the past 3 years, said, "I think Macon County and the Town of Franklin worked really well together in preparing for this event. Everyone was so complimentary and grateful to the Town for hosting a free event for the eclipse. Several people commented that the reason they chose Franklin was because of the free Solar Eclipse event and the Town's website detailing all the events during the eclipse."

The top questions the town staff were asked:

**Where should we eat?
Where can we stay?
Where should we explore?**

IT WAS SO MEMORABLE TO SPEND THIS HISTORIC OCCASION WITH SEVERAL THOUSAND NEW FRIENDS!

Several shopkeepers mentioned how happy and courteous the out of town guests were. Anticipation was high. The visiting "alien" and Llama in costume brought many smiles.

One tourist on Main Street shared, "The hospitality shown to strangers during this event makes our family want to visit Franklin again for our next vacation."

At 2:30 pm traffic was stopped to allow everyone to fill Main Street, literally from one end to the other, to see this spectacular event.

Tony Angel of Tony Angel Media, helped organize this event. When I asked him what kind of response he saw with visitors, he said, "From my experience, our guests were basically stunned that everything we offered was free. I kept hearing, "And it's free?" and "Do you have any more souvenir t-shirts?" We had a map prepared at the information station that showed locations of restaurants, ATMs, restrooms, and other important information. We were more than prepared. Everything was in place and ready for the event from paramedics to law enforcement to the event itself. Folks began arriving on Main Street about 3:00 am to get a parking space, and the Franklin Police Department did an excellent job of making sure they were welcomed."

Summer concluded, "The silence and unity that was felt in the crowd gathered during totality was incredible. It was truly a surreal feeling."

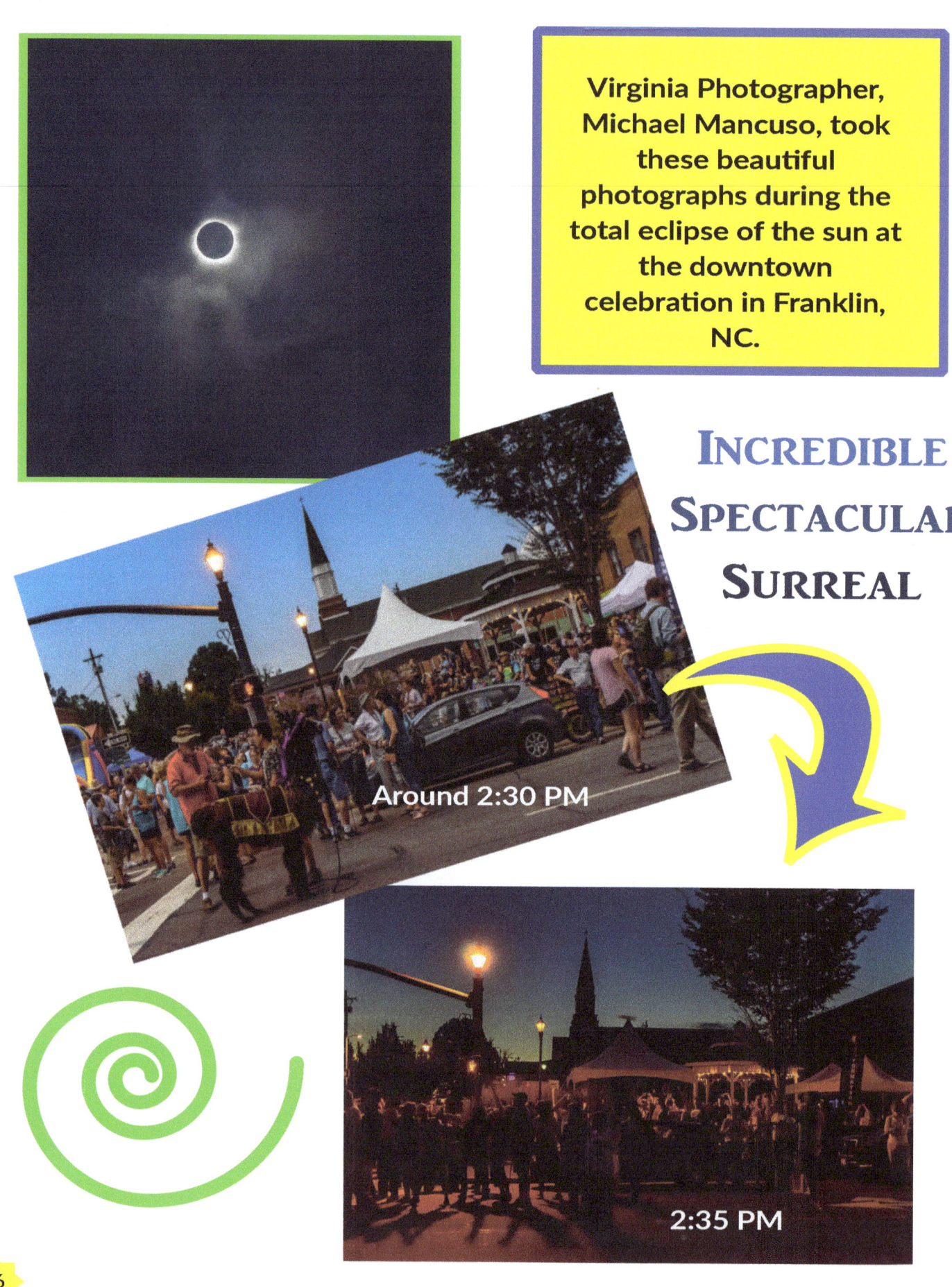

Virginia Photographer, Michael Mancuso, took these beautiful photographs during the total eclipse of the sun at the downtown celebration in Franklin, NC.

## INCREDIBLE
## SPECTACULAR
## SURREAL

Around 2:30 PM

2:35 PM

# Franklin, NC Eclipse details:

Latitude: 35° 10' 56" N | Longitude: 83° 22' 54" W
Partial phase start: 1:06:47PM (EDT), at "1:30 o'clock" on the sun's disk
Duration of Totality: 2m 31s
Totality Start: 2:35:28PM (EDT)
Maximum Eclipse: 2:36:44 PM (EDT
End of Partial Eclipse: 4:00:59 PM (EDT)

### And these comments were received online:

**From New Hampshire:**

"Kudos to a job well done! We drove down from New Hampshire for the fun, and this FB page and the town website were the reason we picked Franklin. Thank you so much for opening your town to us. Excellent atmosphere and hospitality. Well done to the planners and all of the businesses that opened to serve the crowds!"

**From Virginia:**

Thank you Franklin! We drove in from the VA coast, were pleased and impressed with the preparations you'd made for all of us. Activities for the kids, allowance for parking, street closed off, extra food and the all-important potties; tolerance for what must have seemed like a plague of locusts (10k tourists all at once) - thanks again!"

Information and Photos compliments of:
Bob Scott, Summer Woodard, Tony Angel, and Downtown Franklin Shop Owners

# Otto Observatory Gets Exceptional View of the Solar Eclipse

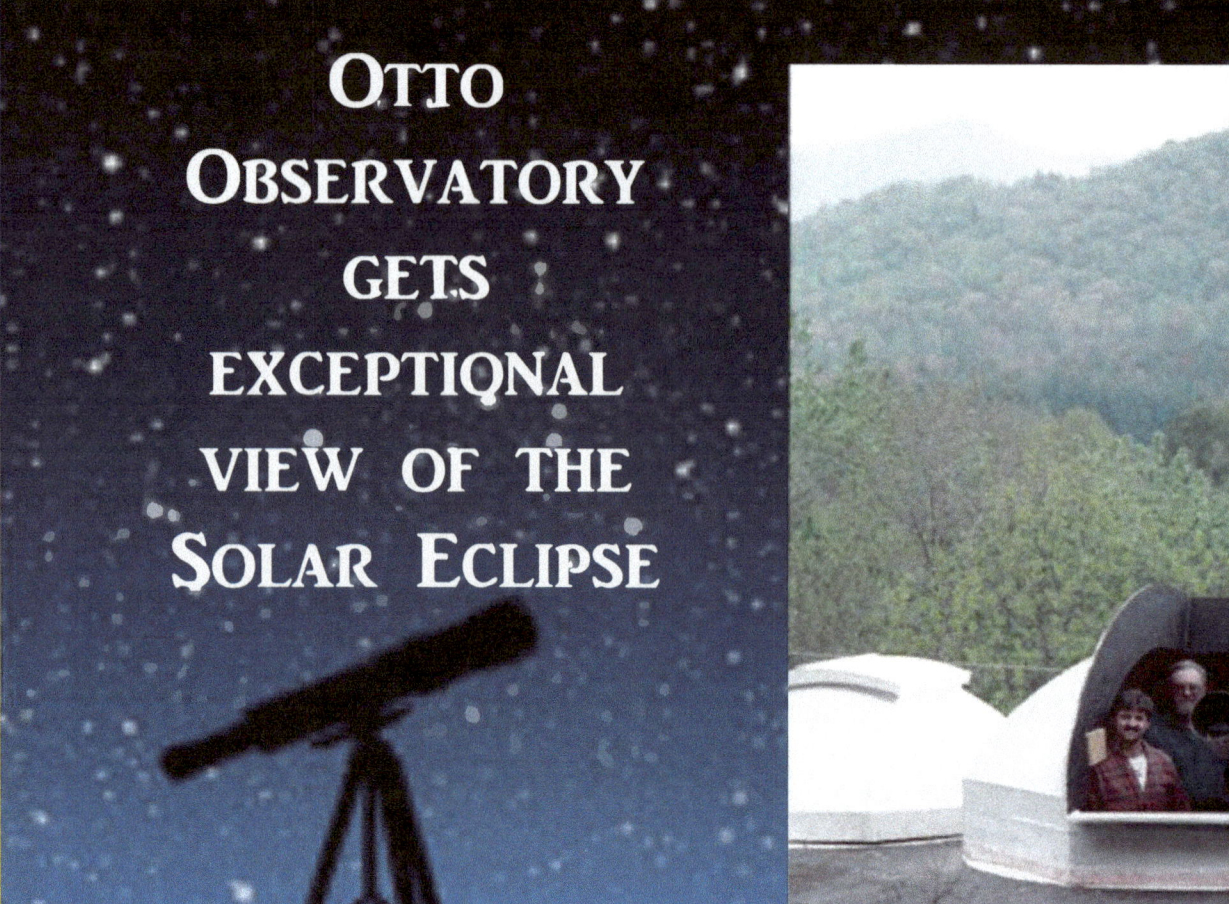

Excerpts taken with permission from
Macon County News- August 30, 2017

Tucked away in Otto, near Coweeta Lab, sits an observatory built nearly 20 years ago by Kevin Kussow and his father, Dave. While the observatory was built in 2000, the 2017 Solar Eclipse served as one of the most historical events in its history.

"My father always had a passion for astronomy though he had his Masters in horticulture," said Kevin. "As a kid he bought us a 6" Newtonian [telescope], and he instilled that passion in me at a very young age. When we moved here to WNC, the skies were much darker than Florida, and we now had an outfitter store that could blend our love of the stars with selling telescopes and astronomy related items. We could introduce others to the wonders of the universe."

Three Eagles no longer sells telescopes, but as the store's owner, Kevin has made contacts with manufacturers over the years that allowed him to purchase several large telescopes for the observatory.

"These are not portable, weighing as much as 300 lbs.", he said. "And require motor driven mounts that can carry these loads and counter the earth's rotation with tremendous accuracy, so the observatory was built. I designed the domes, and it wasn't long before the astrophotography bug hit me hard. It is a Herculean effort to take long exposure photos of the sky without the earth's rotation causing stars, galaxies, Nebula, etc., to look like trailing blurs."

# The 2017 Solar Eclipse served as one of the most historical events in the history of the Observatory.

> "THAT'S WHY YOU TAKE IMAGES, TO TAKE YOU BACK TO THAT MOMENT. THAT'S WHY WE BUILT THE OBSERVATORY, TO SHARE THE MAGNIFICENCE OF OUR UNIVERSE!"
> – KEVIN KUSSOW –

Kevin said it took a few years to dial everything in and learn how it was all done. It required computers and very expensive CCD cameras, but with persistence and many sleepless nights, he became very good at it.

Kevin and his father built the observatory in Otto, and Kevin has spent the last 17 years studying the night's sky and even hosting school groups and others on the property. The facility has two domes and several telescopes ranging in size from 4" to 7" refractors, to 8" to 18" reflectors.

"We often talked about the eclipse of 2017, and how the observatory was dead center of totality," said Kevin. "Unfortunately, my dad passed away last year, but I can assure you he was with me last Monday and weeks prior as I knocked the dust off and prepared for the three-hour shoot."

Kevin said that the decision to attempt to photograph the Eclipse brought immense pressure, but the experience itself was something too great to define with words.

"I've never experienced a total eclipse, words fail at this point," he said.

"We each had our hands full to get the images we shot, just glad the cloud bank stopped just short of blocking our images," said Kevin. "It truly was an awe inspiring event, and I'm sure others will never forget. And that's why you take images, to take you back to that moment. That's why we built the observatory, to share the magnificence of our universe. I will have photos for sale at Three Eagles, I hope by Friday, as I opted to go with a professional lab to ensure the quality of these images."

> "I'VE NEVER EXPERIENCED A TOTAL ECLIPSE, WORDS FAIL AT THIS POINT."
> – KEVIN KUSSOW –

# Franklin, North Carolina

## Chamber of Commerce
## New Location
## Eclipse Celebration

In June of 2017, The Franklin Area Chamber of Commerce moved into its new home at 98 Hyatt Road in the Holly Springs Plaza. Executive Director, Linda Harbuck said that she had no idea the Solar Eclipse would raise so much interest. All summer they received calls requesting information. Most of the motels, cabins and Bed and Breakfasts were booked far in advance. The Chamber started with 1000 pairs of eclipse glasses but gave all of them away before July 1. They had to place three more orders for a total of 10,000 glasses in all. They made sure to buy certified, NASA approved glasses. The last order arrived in Asheville, NC on the Saturday before the Eclipse on Monday. Special Projects Director, Cindy Cavender, made the 90 minute drive to Asheville to pick up the order because there was no Fed Ex delivery from Asheville to Franklin on Saturday or Sunday. It was crucial that the Chamber get these glasses because there were none available anywhere in the area by then. People were beginning to panic because they could not find eclipse glasses. The last order of 5000 glasses was gone before the Eclipse on Monday at 2:36 p.m.

The staff and volunteers grilled hot dogs and provided chips for the approximately 1000 guests in the Holly Springs Plaza Parking lot. Linda said there was a feeling of excitement and anticipation in the air leading up to the Total Eclipse; however, during the actual Eclipse, there was total silence as everyone watched in amazement. A bird's eye view from our own front yard !

**THERE WAS TOTAL SILENCE AS EVERYONE WATCHED IN AMAZEMENT!**

DJ, George Young, from Radio WFSC/WNCC played eclipse, sun, and moon tunes for the crowd leading up to the Eclipse. The weather was perfect and there was building excitement.

Official Chamber photographer, Eric Haggart was able to get pictures of stages of the eclipse as it progressed, which he later turned into the beautiful composite seen in this book.

Chamber Administrative Assistant, Diane Baldwin was a little surprised that there was not more traffic as the eclipse approached, but afterward, it seemed like everyone tried to leave at the same time, and there was a huge traffic jam in all directions.
Linda said that the eclipse brought a lot of visitors and business to our town. Many visitors went away with numerous Franklin eclipse souvenirs to cherish and pass along to their children, grandchildren, and even great-grandchildren as they tell them about seeing this wonderful Total Solar Eclipse while in Franklin, North Carolina. Wouldn't it be great for Franklin if we could special order another total eclipse for 2018?

New Location opened June 1, 2017

Chamber pictures by Eric Haggart

# Macon County Library Celebrates and Educates

The Macon County Public Library spent months preparing for their Solar Eclipse viewing party. They, along with the other libraries in the Fontana Regional Library system, applied for and received a grant to purchase an inflatable planetarium.

This was very popular, and they were able to show in advance what the Great American Total Eclipse would be like. They ordered approximately 4000 pairs of eclipse glasses and gave out a limited amount each day, as the eclipse approached.

They prepared for up to 1000 guests to attend their viewing event. They had a food truck and a Lunt LS60 THaPT Solar telescope for people to get a close-up view and eclipse crafts for children to make.

On the day of the event, their parking lot was full and around 800 people were there to share this special day at the Library. As it turned out, the Macon County Public Library was one of the few viewing places to have any NASA approved eclipse glasses for their patrons to wear. People viewing in other locations came and picked up eclipse glasses. They became a precious commodity in Macon County and around the United States! Companies could not keep up with the demand for them.

Our NASA subject matter expert assists with safe viewing

This is what Children's Librarian, Cristen Dando, had to say about their event:

"I had just as much fun watching the people during the Eclipse as I did watching the actual eclipse. It was great seeing everyone so excited, especially the kids.

People lined up at the library to use the telescope that was set up. They shared their eclipse glasses. They showed each other the cool shadows.

I have always loved science, so for me, it was great to see others excited about it too!"

*I have always loved science, so for me, it was great to see others excited about it also!*

# It was a great day at the Library!

Car with eclipse leaf shadows

After their viewing party was over, Macon County Public Library collected eclipse glasses for the Franklin Girl Scouts. Other people in town brought in glasses. After a while they had to say, "Enough! We are done."

The glasses will be sent overseas to the next total eclipse site, so children there can safely experience a total eclipse!

24

# Entegra Bank's Eclipse Event 2017

Since Entegra Bank has always given back to the community, when we found out that we would be in the path of totality, we decided to do a big event for everyone. Planning began in November 2016. Entegra Bank's Spectacular Solar Eclipse Event was held in the fields below the Corporate Center, and we had a perfect viewing area.

We had plenty of parking available and probably had 1500-1800 people come to our event. We gave away Mini Moon Pies, popcorn, drinks, moon rock stress balls, glow in the dark tattoos, color changing cups and bracelets, hand fans and of course, the solar glasses.

We had people from all over North Carolina, Virginia, Florida, and as far away as Washington, California, Mexico, and Canada. Our international visitors included people from Bolivia, Greece and a gentleman from Serbia. He flew to Washington, DC and drove down to Franklin just to watch the eclipse! Families gathered with their children. There was a monk in his robes who met up with five of his friends to view the eclipse. There were photographers with their Nikons and Canons set up, ready for the big event.

It was a beautiful day but hot, and most of the crowd stayed under the tent. At first contact, a lot of the people came out to see the start of the eclipse, but went back under the shade until closer to the time of totality.

About 2:25pm, 10 minutes before the totality, we started getting some light clouds. We could see a bright star over Franklin as the afternoon sort of turned a little darker, like it does when there are heavy rain clouds. The color of the grass and people's clothing changed, becoming duller. The lights came on at the Franklin House. The total eclipse was getting close.

There was a photographer next to me who had one camera pointed at the roof of our white tent. We looked for the shadow bands to show up on the tent, but with the clouds we couldn't see anything. I turned and looked through the tent towards Sylva, and the mountains were dark. I turned back towards the sun, and it went dark. That quick! So this was totality! I wasn't expecting that. I thought it would be more of a gradual darkening, kind of like a regular night fall. From what I understand, the moon's shadow races across the land at about 2,000 miles per hour, and that is why it got dark that quick.

We saw a small plane flying around south of us. It was above the clouds, and I thought...man, that guy has the best view of all! Bet he got some good pictures from up there!

We were not wearing our glasses since the sun was covered by the clouds, but you could still see the total eclipse. Some people had taken pictures with filters on their phone cameras with the clouds, but you couldn't see any of the eclipse. We did not see the Diamond Ring effect or the Bailey's Beads which were things I was looking forward to experiencing. But during that 2 minutes and 30 seconds, it was awesome!

Traffic stopped moving. People were talking in whispers, in awe of this incredible sight. Time seemed to have come to a standstill. There was an eerie feeling, that things were not a normal dusk or dawn, but not something I could put a finger on. And we were in a large group of people who were experiencing the same thing, and they could not describe it either. There was so much to experience during the totality, and it is something you really have to see for yourself. People can describe it any number of ways, but it doesn't really capture the feelings, emotions, the effect it has on you. Reverent. Calmness. Beauty. Joy. All rolled into one.

**PEOPLE WERE TALKING IN WHISPERS, IN AWE OF THIS INCREDIBLE SIGHT!**

# What an experience, the wonder of it all!

There were no crickets chirping where we were, but I've heard others that were not at our event say they heard crickets chirping, roosters crowing, dogs that went into hiding, and even bats that came out for a short period of time.

And then, the sunlight came back. Back to reality. What an experience, the wonder of it all! So much to take in, and you didn't have enough time to process it.

A friend of mine who works at the airport told me later that the airport had filled up. A lot of people flew in just to see the eclipse. Of course with a wide open field at the airport, it probably was a very good viewing place. She told me about the last plane that arrived right before the eclipse, and she had to turn him away because they were full. I wondered if it was the small plane we saw flying around above the clouds.

We were really lucky that Franklin had such a long time in totality. Imagine if it were only for 30 seconds. The next time Franklin will be in the path of totality will be in 136 years from now. And it will only last 28 seconds.

**Eye witness account by:**
**Deanna Wagner**
**Head of Marketing**
**Corporate Office**
**Entegra Bank**
**Franklin, NC**

When the Eclipse was over, East bound traffic towards Asheville was backed up for hours!

## Fun Facts:

Entegra ordered: 5040 Moon Pies, and 10,000 glasses

The parking lot was full of mostly Virginia License Plates.

The bank started working on this event 10 months in advance!

# Excerpts from the Nantahala Ranger District Solar Eclipse Report

### Michael L. Wilkins, District Ranger

Every ranger and employee of the Nantahala District was on duty the day of the Great American Solar Eclipse. A plan was formulated to spread personnel around to key locations within the Nantahala District and ensure that the public remained safe. A combination of hand-held radios and cell phones were used to keep in touch.

**These are the locations that were most used and the number of cars parked at each one:**

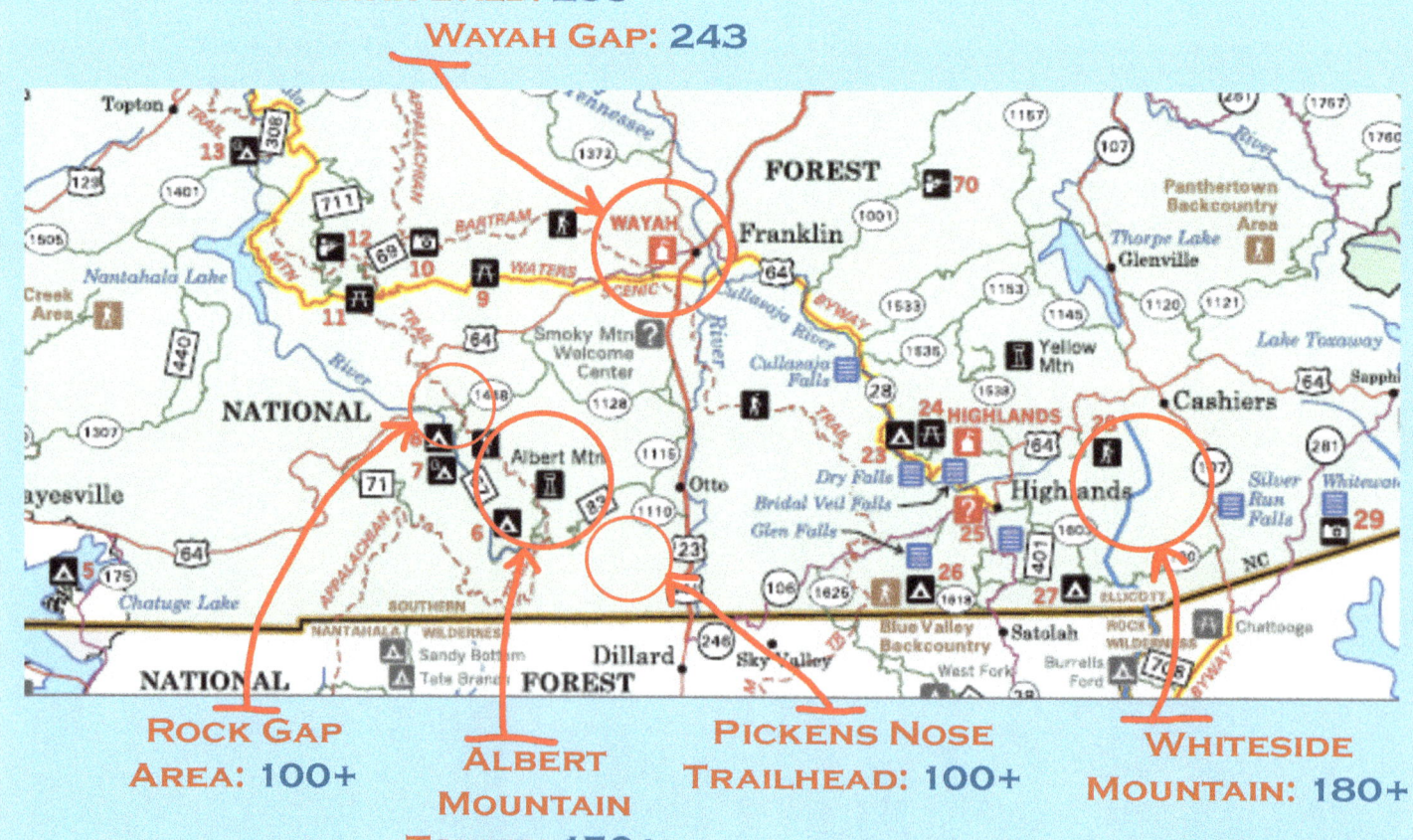

- **Wayah Bald:** 255
- **Wayah Gap:** 243
- **Rock Gap Area:** 100+
- **Albert Mountain Tower:** 150+
- **Pickens Nose Trailhead:** 100+
- **Whiteside Mountain:** 180+

**Subtotal: 866+ cars counted**

Hurricane Primitive Camp had campers on about every square inch of the grassy areas. Tellico Gap trailhead and road had a long line of cars going east and west. Roadside camping was heavy in Blue Valley, Standing Indian Basin and along the River Road.

While we expected everyone to want to get to the mountain tops, we were still surprised by the turn out to places like Albert Mountain and Pickens Nose. The 120 tents 2 miles from the road on Sunday night at the field on Siler Bald, Tellico Gap, and Winding Stair Gap were also a surprise.

It was the general feeling by all those in the field that our presence at the sites and along multiple dead-end single lane roads helped facilitate a safe outcome and positive behavior by 99% of our visitors. Our public servants at ALL locations received multiple "thank yous" from the public. We had no known accidents or incidents other than issues with towing a few vehicles blocking traffic and a few vehicles off the downhill road bank who had passed their ability to get back up on the Forest Service Road.

The hardest part was the number of viewers trying to leave at the same time. There was a full range of Eclipse expressions, from tears of joy to tin foil hats. However, those in attendance treated our forest well. The cleanup crew at Siler Bald mentioned that they did not find one scrap of trash at the Siler Bald makeshift campsite. 120 tents and not one scrap of trash.

That is the kind of Nantahala forest guests who are welcome back any time!

# The Cowee School Arts & Heritage Center

The 14th Annual Franklin Area Folk Festival, "A Celebration of Appalachian Heritage", was held at Cowee School the Saturday before The Great American Eclipse.

Due to expected increase of eclipse tourists in the area that weekend, shuttles ran between downtown and Cowee School and extra porta johns were leased. Eclipse glasses, books and eclipse-themed jewelry were for sale, in addition to all of the regular heritage crafts. It was a great day, which left the work crew exhausted, so nothing was formally organized at the school for the actual day of the eclipse. However, Cowee School hosts a concert series every year. And the much requested Becky Buller Band from neighboring Tennessee was scheduled to perform at Cowee School the following month. At the concert, Becky shared that during the Great American Solar Eclipse, she and award winning banjo player, Ned Luberecki, had donned their glasses, looked up at the sky and played the very appropriate, "You Are My Sunshine"!

## "YOU ARE MY SUNSHINE, MY ONLY SUNSHINE"

# The Franklin Press
Established 1886

## Eclipse brought 10,000 visitors, revenue to town    by Ryan Hanchett    December 8, 2017

It is impossible to quantify what a once-in-a-lifetime cosmic event meant to Macon County, but the early numbers are in and it's clear that both the county and the Town of Franklin benefitted from the Great American Solar Eclipse. Franklin was in the path of totality for the Aug. 21 eclipse and celestial observers snatched up hotel rooms well in advance of the event.

"We estimated that we had 10,000 people come to Franklin for the eclipse and we came to that number based on crowd estimates at eclipse-related events, traffic counts and several other factors," Franklin Mayor Bob Scott said. "It was a great day for the town in terms of exposure for all of the great things we have to offer visitors and also in terms of a revenue bump."

Occupancy tax collections in Franklin were up more than 16 percent for August 2017 compared to August 2016. The town collected $15,268 in occupancy tax in August, compared to $12,801 last year.

Because the eclipse was late in the month, Franklin Chamber of Commerce Director Linda Harbuck noted that some of the additional occupancy tax revenue was not collected until September, a fact that is borne out by the numbers.

A total of $14,815 in occupancy tax was collected in Franklin in September. That number represents a 21-percent increase over the $11,754 collected in September 2016.

The numbers associated with the county's share of the occupancy tax also show a boom in September. The county collected $21,215 in September 2017 compared to $17,623 in the same month year prior, despite the county's August occupancy tax collections being roughly equal from 2016 ($22,209) to 2017 ($21,388).

Macon County also realized a slight uptick in sales tax for August. The county collected $823,954 in sales tax in 2017, compared to $821,363 year prior.

Aside from the initial fiscal benefits, Scott noted that the eclipse will pay dividends for years to come if and when those guests who came on Aug. 21 make a return trip to the area.

"I was in Cary recently and I struck up a conversation with a nice lady working in a cafeteria and when I mentioned I was from Franklin she said that she and her boyfriend had come to Franklin for the eclipse," Scott said. "What was most encouraging was that she told me they really enjoyed the area and they are planning to come back next spring."

Scott believes that the eclipse was the biggest single day in the town's history in terms of tourist visitation.

"We had reports of it taking more than two hours to get from Franklin to Sylva after the eclipse," Scott said. "I think it's safe to say that has never happened before, and the traffic going toward Clayton (Georgia) was just as thick. To have so many people come to Franklin and take part in the eclipse without having any major issues was a real tribute to all of the hard work that our staff put in to making that day a success."

Reprinted with permission from The Franklin Press

# Part Two: Smaller Gatherings in the Franklin Area

## Photographed by Kevin DeLoach

The Supermoon picture was handheld from my back porch while using my crutches, after knee surgery, to turn myself into a tripod. It was shot using the same Canon 7D, Canon Ultrasonic 100-300 lens, at ISO 100, f/5.6, at 1/125 sec. This lens has Image Stabilization. Otherwise, there would be no way possible to hand hold a shot at 300mm @ a 1/125 sec exposure and get a crisp image.

Kevin

## Carringer Farms

## It Was an Experience I Will Never Forget!

Don and Belinda Carringer of Carringer Farms, 2206 Mountain Grove Rd, Franklin had a quiet eclipse viewing on their farm. Don has been farming all of his life and sells produce at the Franklin and Sylva Farmers Markets and also to a few local restaurants.

Belinda specializes in producing jams, jellies and relishes, sourdough bread, potted plants and whipped honey. They also have a large flock of hens and sell their eggs locally. The Carringers are a vital part of making the local foods movement a reality in our area.
And they always greet their customers with a smile.

Belinda had this to say about the eclipse, " I sat on our porch to watch the eclipse and observed everything going on around us before, during, and after. Before, the birds were chirping and the chickens were making their clucking noises. During the eclipse, it felt like the whole world was quiet and still. The birds ceased to chirp, and the hens all filed into their houses. Afterwards, the lone rooster we have started crowing, and the rest of the hens came back outside. It was an experience I'll never forget."

IT FELT LIKE THE WHOLE WORLD WAS QUIET AND STILL.

# TRULY A SIGHT TO BEHOLD !

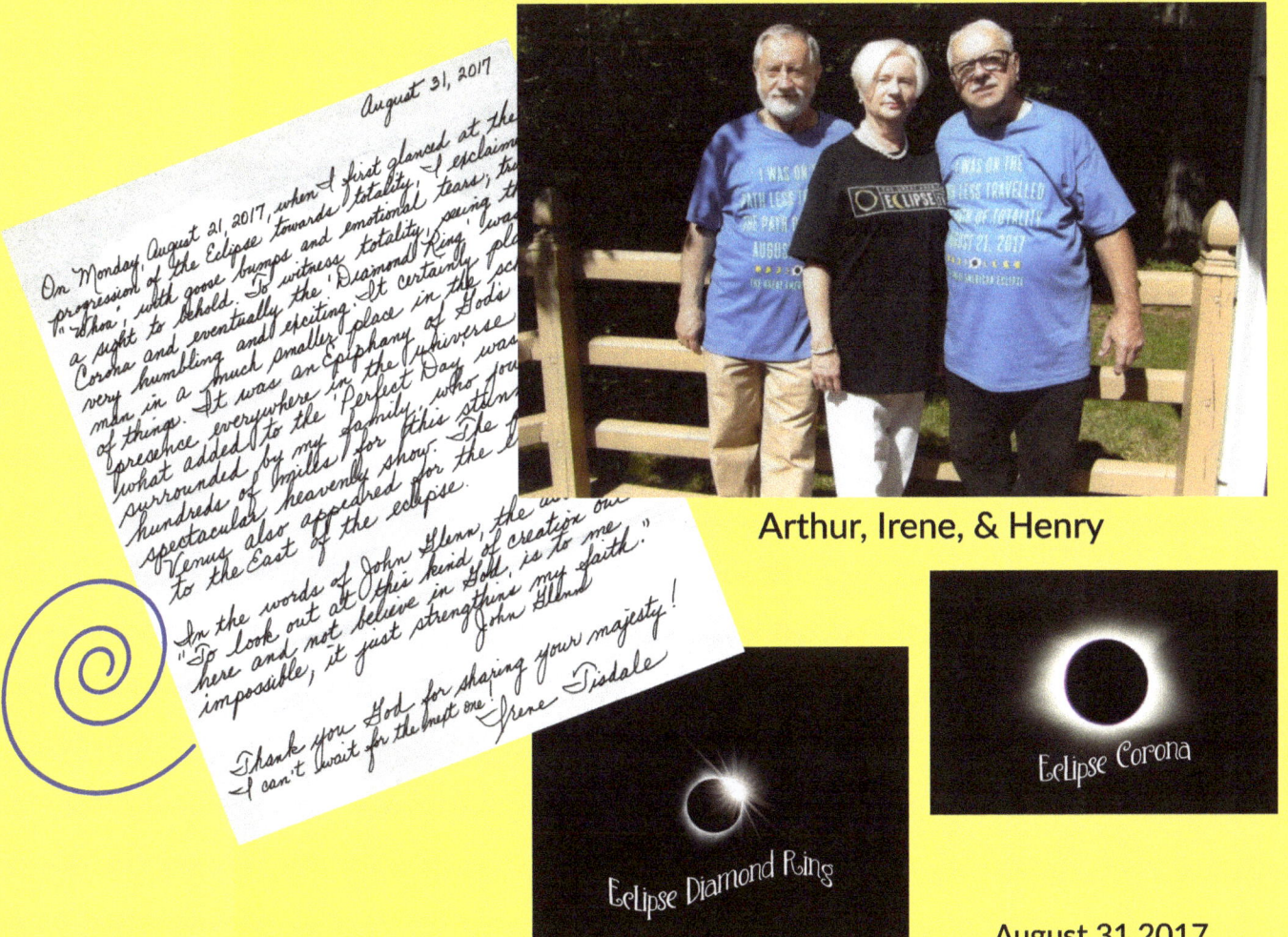

Arthur, Irene, & Henry

August 31, 2017

On Monday, August 21, 2017, when I first glanced at the progression of the Eclipse towards totality, I exclaimed, "Whoa", with goose bumps and emotional tears; truly a sight to behold. To witness totality, seeing the Corona and eventually the 'Diamond Ring' was very humbling and exciting. It certainly places man in a much smaller place in the scheme of things. It was an Epiphany of God's loving presence everywhere in the universe. And what added to the 'Perfect Day' was being surrounded by my family, who journeyed hundreds of miles for this stunning, spectacular heavenly show. The planet Venus also appeared for the event, just to the east of the eclipse.

In the words of John Glenn, the astronaut, "To look out at this kind of creation out here and not believe in God, is to me impossible, it just strengthens my faith."
                                              John Glenn

Thank you God for sharing your majesty! I can't wait for the next one!

Firsthand account by: *Irene Tisdale*

# OBSERVABLE COSMIC EVENT IN REAL TIME

At the time I didn't realize it, but I was seeing actual heavenly bodies in motion. We experience the gradual effects of the sun and moon along with the earth's rotation. This was an observable cosmic event in real time. My photo's of the eclipse ended up being just a record and did not capture the subtle colors I saw. So I painted a watercolor to try to recreate what the camera had missed.

Firsthand account by:
*John Sill*

One of the things that impressed me about the eclipse was the shimmery blue of the corona. I expected it to be gold. The icy fire surrounding the darkened sun totally mesmerized me. I couldn't take my eyes off it to notice anything else. I do remember the gasps of awe from the friends surrounding me as we shared the event. I think we were witnessing a brief preview of heaven.

Firsthand account by:
*Cathryn Sill*

*The icy fire surrounding the darkened sun totally mesmerized me.*

Ah Lord GOD! Behold, You have made the heavens and the earth by Your great power and outstretched arm.
There is nothing too hard for You.
Jeremiah 32:17 NKJV

Eclipse Watercolor painting by John Sill

# At the Old Family Farm out on Potts Branch

Sybil Potts Cabe Major and some of her family were visiting her son and daughter in law, Ron and Laura Cabe, at their old family farm out on Potts Branch.

Sybil had always been a hard working woman. In years past she grew corn and wheat on the bottomlands of the Cowee Valley, where Potts Creek flows into the Little Tennessee River, right across from the old Hall farm.

Sybil had visited 49 countries and every state in the union and raised three adventurous sons, but she was still very excited that the Great American Solar Eclipse that would be passing right over their farm!

The evening before the eclipse, all the family went out to dinner. Her son, Ron, who is famous in Franklin for growing very hearty Shitake Mushrooms and selling them at the Franklin Farmers Market, took 3 bites of his dinner, grabbed his chest and said: "Call the ambulance." Formerly a competitive surfer, he has always appeared to be the picture of health, so this was quite a surprise.

While Ron waited in the Owen Heart Tower of Mission Hospital for the doctors to perform surgery, he urged his family to go home and enjoy the eclipse. With some reservations, they left and headed back to Cowee.

"Call the ambulance!"

Maps provided by MyTopo.com

The day of the Eclipse, Sybil was standing out on the deck at about 2:15 with her grandson. She could feel the wind rushing down from the Nantahala Range, as the time drew closer.

Although she missed Ron terribly, she was so content to be on the farmstead that day, looking out over the valley. The eclipse was incredible. As the sky grew darker, Sybil could hear the crickets chirping and feel the wind blowing.

It was another once-in-a-lifetime experience to be notched into the belt of this well-seasoned traveler and devoted matriarch.

Ron did get to watch the partial eclipse from his hospital window and was thankful to be alive.

He has since recovered from his surgery and is back at the Franklin Farmers market again, looking more fit and chipper than ever. But he confided in me one day when I was picking up my mushrooms, "You know, I have a hard time keeping up with my 90-year-old Mother!" Having spent some time with Sybil, I believe it.

THE OLD FAMILY FARM OUT ON POTTS BRANCH

*She could feel the wind rushing down from the Nantahala Range.*

# Eclipse Gathering at the Suminski Farmette

Events that draw family and friends together are worth putting effort into. An eclipse is most certainly an event. It takes some planning and patience to fully enjoy the spectacle in the sky. A small gathering of family and friends joined up at the Suminski Family Farmette to strategize in preparation for the eclipse. Lunch was enjoyed, viewing glasses distributed, lawn chairs and blankets gathered, cameras prepared and more.

We meandered out to the viewing area that opened perfectly through the trees to the clear sky above. We laid out the food and set up our individual viewing "stations". Viewing glasses here, food plate there and drink under there. We laid out a large white sheet so we could view the shadow snakes and chattered about the other events associated with the eclipse. "What do you think the animals will do?", "Do you know about the diamond ring?", "How about Baileys Beads?" We all felt the mounting anticipation of what was about to occur right on our little farmette.

As the moon made its way across the face of the sun, the conversation was happy and full of wonder at such a humbling experience, in awe of God's creation. Joy, wonder, awe, love, and humility mixed with tidbits of science were all felt and expressed in our little group. As totality approached, Frankie the cat sprinted to the house, bugs and birds chirped and whistled, fooled by the increasing darkness. Our chickens went to roost, the roosters crowed and the goats bedded down. With totality, we shed our glasses and vocalized the wonder and joy we felt with "oohs" and "ahhs" from each of us as some particular phenomenon would catch our attention. We were fully invested in the moment we were experiencing. Once the eclipse ended we wished it hadn't and hoped we didn't miss anything. We packed up our eclipse kit and headed back across the road fully satisfied and in awe of our Father, God the Creator.

Firsthand account by: *Joe Suminski*

**AS THE MOON MADE ITS WAY ACROSS THE FACE OF THE SUN THE CONVERSATION WAS HAPPY AND FULL OF WONDER AT SUCH A HUMBLING EXPERIENCE, IN AWE OF GOD'S CREATION.**

# Crickets, Cookies, and Cat on the Run

The residents of Cowee Mountain Valley Farm and guests had an eclipse viewing party complete with eclipse ginger- mallow cookies. I had been downtown earlier in the day, doing a book signing at "Books Unlimited for Kids" for our latest book, "Cowee Sam and the Solar Eclipse." Downtown was packed, and the air was charged with anticipation of the eclipse. I have never seen so many out of towners! And every single person seemed so happy to be in our little town. It was exhilarating.

I headed home at 1:00 pm, wondering if the roads would be jammed. But once past the downtown bridge construction, the roads were very clear. Upon arriving home, I joined the party of family and friends, down by the river and got settled into my chair. Everyone was talking and laughing. They were too excited to eat any snacks, until later. As the light began to dim, the chickens headed home to roost and the goats followed. There was a 360-degree orange and pink sunset. Several in our party had their cell phones set to alert us to the moment of totality, so that we could take off our glasses. Just when the alarms went off, a horn blew in the distance, and we heard a crowd cheering, possibly from downtown. Our cat, Frankie, ran as fast as he could, like a black streak of lightning, up to our house. Traffic on 441 went silent, the daytime birds and bugs stopped making noises and were replaced with the evening sound of crickets chirping. Some of us put on our sweaters, even though it was 3:30 in the afternoon on a hot August day!

Fireworks went off over by the Lake Emory Dam. It was spectacular, and for me time and space seemed suspended. I thought that only our Heavenly father could figure out the exact timing and distance between the sun, Earth, and moon, which would allow His children, watching from the surface of planet Earth, to be able to see this. I said a quiet prayer of gratitude and thought about how blessed I was to be surrounded by loved ones. It was amazing! And then, before we knew it, the diamond ring appeared, cell phone alarms went off again, and we put our glasses back on. There was a 360-degree sunrise, traffic began to move, birds began to chirp, and our rooster crowed. For us, the eclipse was over.

Firsthand account by:
*Claire Suminski*

# Dorothy Deal & Opal Brown
# Lifelong Friends on Mashburn Branch Road

Dorothy Deal and Opal Brown both moved into their houses on Mashburn Branch Road, as newly married brides, over 60 years ago. They are still friends and neighbors today. Dorothy's maiden name was Angel. Her people had settled that area, and she attended the Mashburn Branch one-room school house as a youngster. When the old school was torn down, the Mashburn Branch Baptist Church was built in its place and became the center of their community. This is what happened at each of their homes the day of the eclipse.

Dorothy Deal said that as the time approached for the Total Eclipse of the sun, she and her son, David, were out in the yard sitting at the picnic table snapping beans. One of her granddaughters was following the eclipse countdown on her cell phone and reporting progress to her grandmother.

Dorothy said she could see a big, black cloud coming and "smack", it hit right at the time of the eclipse! They thought it was neat that the sky got dark, but their chickens did not seem to notice one bit. Dorothy's granddaughter told them to stop working and look up when the phase of totality started. They could not see very much, and Dorothy hollered out, "That darn cloud has ruined our view!"

Just down the road, Opal Brown was out in the yard watching the moon move towards the sun. Her son, Lamon, could see a black cloud moving in from over by Highlands. Would they be able to see the eclipse? Right at 2:30, the cloud moved in front of the sun. Opal let out an exasperated sigh and said, "Now that's just disgustin'!" All of that commotion for nothing! Her son did notice that the crickets started chirping the minute the sky went dark and fireworks and some bottle rockets were shot off nearby. Both of them had a hard time believing that people drove as far as they did to watch the eclipse in Macon County. But in the end, they all concluded that they were glad to be a part of this historic event, even if that black cloud did get in the way!

*"That darn cloud ruined our view, but I was glad to be a part of it anyway."*
*-Dorothy Deal*

Mashburn Branch School circa 1948

# A Shadow show during the Eclipse

We spent Eclipse Day 2017 at home enjoying the celestial show! Fortunately, the clouds parted at the right time, and we were able to witness this wonderful event in full. The most interesting things that we saw were the crescent shadows on our driveway. Our cats, Miko & Rosie, seemed to be very confused by the sudden darkness and drop in temperature. They enjoyed watching the shadows change, too!

Our business, Swoon the Bakery, made some festive decorated sugar cookies and moon & stars cupcakes for our local farmers market!

"The most interesting things that we saw were the crescent shadows on our driveway!"

Firsthand account by:
*The Elliott Family*

Miko and Rosie, our cats, enjoyed watching the shadows change too!

# A Light and Shadow Show

Susan Ervin and Bill McLarney live in an open valley along the Little Tennessee River. They very much looked forward to watching the eclipse from their property with beautiful sky views.

Here are some of Susan's observations during the 180-degree sunset right before totality and the "shadow show" that followed:

"The light was very different from a normal sunset. It seemed sort of green and shadows were much clearer, no doubt because the light was coming through at a different angle than usual. Everything got very still--no bird calls and even no breeze. The most amazing part was the shadows of the crescent sun projected through openings in the leaf canopy and through other openings. The most striking being, little crescent suns projected through every opening in the latticework on the side of our house and hundreds of crescents on the porch floor. They were also projected onto the side of the house in some places and on the ground under trees. The temperature dropped over 10 degrees. It didn't get totally dark outside, but inside one would have had to turn on lights to see."

Bill and Susan's guests enjoyed BLTs and home-churned ice cream during their eclipse get together. It took their Winston Salem guests nearly 8 hours to return home after the eclipse (normally a 4-hour drive). Susan summed the event up by saying, "My 95-year-old father was enchanted, as were we all."

Bill holds a Doctorate in Fisheries from the University of Michigan but considers himself an Aquatic Conservation Biologist. Since 1989, Bill has conducted Index of Biotic Integrity Surveys on fish populations in the Upper Little Tennessee Watershed. Susan is an avid gardener and actively involved with Cowee School and the Women's History Trail. Both Bill and Susan have a great love of the outdoors.

Firsthand account by:
*Susan Ervin*

# Winding Stair Farm and Nursery

Winding Stair Farm sits below the headwaters of the Nantahala River. The farm practices sustainable, organic farming and provides heirloom vegetables, free-range eggs, and humanely raised sheep and chickens to the community. The owners were very excited about the eclipse and ended up hosting 60 people at Winding Stair Farm.

Michelle, who is an owner and the full-time manager of the farm, shared, "A few of us sat in the pasture with our sheep and chickens. Others sat by the Nantahala River. The most incredible part was listening to the sounds of the farm changing with the increasing darkness. One of the joys of farming is experiencing the land at different times of the day throughout the year, and observing and enjoying the changes in light and animal behavior. The Total Eclipse added an unforgettable layer to this whole journey!"

Since the eclipse, the Farm has expanded to include a beautiful nursery, located on 57 Saunders Road, just outside Franklin. The owners invite you to come visit and check it out!

*The total eclipse added an unforgettable layer to this whole journey!*

# Part Three: Gatherings West of the Franklin Area

### Photographed by Kevin DeLoach

The Orange Diamond was shot with the Canon 7D, Canon Ultrasonic 100-300 lens, at ISO 800, f/5.6, at 1/250 sec. This one was shot with a solar filter installed, thus the orange cast, to protect my camera... and eyes.     ~ Kevin

# Selected Fun Solar Eclipse Facts of the Day
*reprinted with permission from GreatAmericanEclipse.com*

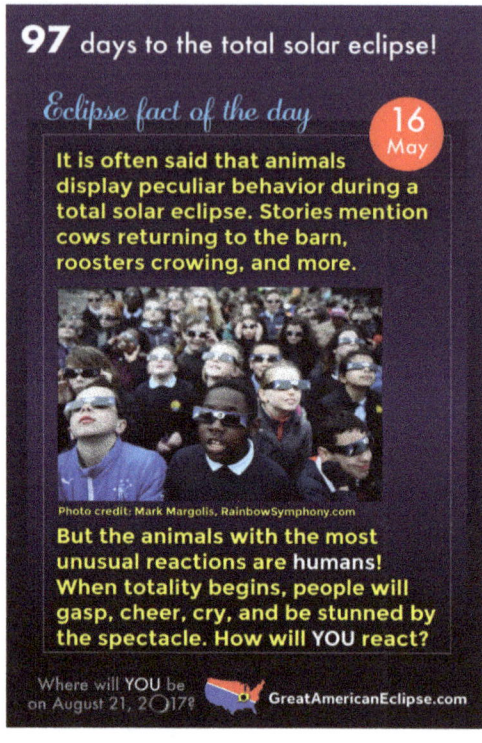

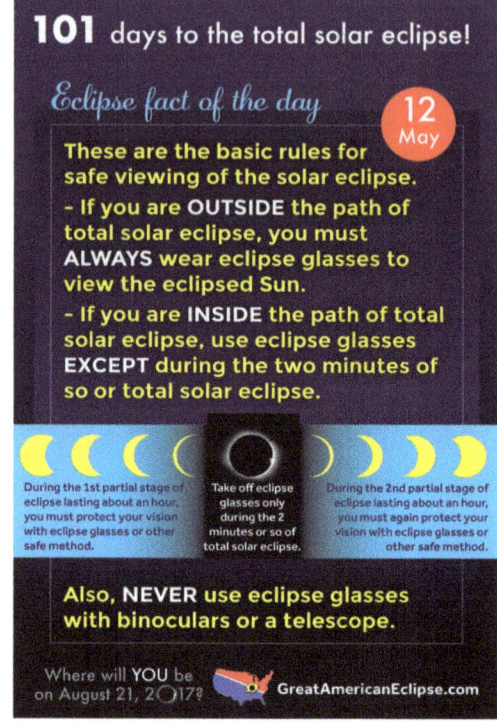

# The town of Andrews made a once-in-a-lifetime experience visitors will never forget!

Reprinted by permission of The Andrews Journal
News section, page 4, Kandy Barnard Journaling  August 31, 2017

I am among many to be amazed at how the people in the Town of Andrews efficiently took care of so many visitors during the Great American Total Solar Eclipse. The three-day festival downtown was like something you would see in Gatlinburg, Tenn. From shuttle buses to the wares of more than 80 vendors, there was something for everyone. All of you worked hard and it paid off, but more important, you made a once-in-a-lifetime experience a memory our visitors will never forget.

The fact that NASA placed Andrews on their website for the total eclipse put Andrews on the map, and Andrews Middle School was the chosen spot to collect data. Amber Ledford, who teaches science at the school, said, "We had a dark field which is where the scientist set up camp, so nothing could interfere with their collection of important data."

The four NASA scientists from Johnson Space Center in Texas set up camp in the eastern section of the dark/ working field beside the National Geographic group. U.S. Forest Service Southern Research Station agents Michael Robinson and Jeremy Jones were actually working for the government, imaging the eclipse and taking readings on multiple instruments before, during, and after the eclipse.

There also were scientists from Penn State, Appalachian State, Duke and Michael Overacker with the Mobile Astronomy Outreach program in Roanoke, Va., all of whom camped in the dark field.

Dave Talon and Drew Smith, David Heflin, Sam Hanessian, Amber Ledford and Alaina Ledford standing by telescope

The "teaching team" consisted of Drew Smith from NASA Marshall Flight Center, Dave Talon, retired government official/astronomer, and David Heflin, retired USDA and astronomer with Crystal Coast Star Gazers. They set up their telescopes and were willing to show their images and teach astronomy to anyone interested. They had an EQ 114 on a Celestron CG-5 mount telescope and an Orion 6" Dobsonian. Overacker brought a Hydrogen Alpha telescope, which takes down the brightness of the sun and creates extreme contrast for phenomenal views of the sun. He also had nine other types of telescopes set up for anyone who wanted to look, and he explained them in detail.

The teaching team showed science teachers Amber Ledford and Alaina Ledford how the sun looked on the surface through special sun filters, even showing the sunspots.

During the evening they were able to see Saturn, which was positioned to where you could see the planet, and the complete set of rings and many of the moons. They also viewed Jupiter, which was having atmospheric disturbances, and many of the moons were visible around the planet as well.

**NASA**  *Johnson Space Center*  PENN STATE
**NATIONAL GEOGRAPHIC**  *U.S. Forest Service*
**MOBILE ASTRONOMY OUTREACH**  *Southern Research Station*
APPALACHIAN STATE

THEY SET UP THEIR TELESCOPES AND WERE WILLING TO SHOW THEIR IMAGES AND TEACH ASTRONOMY TO ANYONE INTERESTED.

Duke

In one of the lessons they pointed out the big dipper and the second star in the constellation. All of the scientists were absolutely amazed at how visible the many stars were in this valley.

In one of the lessons they pointed out the big dipper and the second star in the handle of the constellation, (Mizar-Alcor). This star was used by the Romans because there is actually a second star right beside it that is barely visible to the naked eye if you have good vision.

The soldiers who could see this were chosen to be Centurions. To the right of the Big Dipper is the Constellation Cygnus (the swan); if you looked between the two, due North, they were looking in the direction of Tatham Gap on Robbinsville Mountain from the dark field.

The dark/working field was closely monitored by the science teachers, who had to make sure that no headlights, or lights of any kind, were being used, so there would not be any interference with the telescopes. The only color of lights that could be used were red or green.

All of the scientists were absolutely amazed at how visible so many stars were in this valley, and the fact that the sky was so clear they could see bands of the Milky Way. They were even able to see meteors from the Perseid meteor shower and a green ball of fire that actually arched over Andrews Middle.

This article reprinted with permission of the Andrews Journal

## Airport shatters record for landings

Author(s): Kelsey Richardson krichardson@myandrewsjournal.com   Date: August 31, 2017
Section: News

Western Carolina Regional Airport broke its record for the most amount of aircraft at one time, with 136 jets and airplanes landing before the Great American Solar Eclipse.

"At first, we didn't think it was going to be a big deal," aviation service worker Joe Cloer said. "And then we kept getting more and more phone calls, and I realized this is going to be something big."

From a Gulfstream 400 to a Beechcraft King Air, the airport transformed into a static air show with the amount of aircraft flooding into the facility on Aug. 21.

According to some observers, the stars were out as well. Local businessman Charles West said Monday that acclaimed Hollywood director Steven Spielberg was in Andrews along with other stars, but he could not personally confirm the rumors.

Cloer, who was the only full-time staff member working at the event, said two weeks before the eclipse he could barely get any work done because of all the calls. Cloer said he counted around 1,000 phone calls during the days before the eclipse.

Unlike most airports, which were only taking reservations during the eclipse, Andrews was first come, first serve. The easy access allowed people to pop in the day of with only a phone call's notice.

Cloer said the airport only had three days to prepare for the influx of aircraft and people. With the help of Cherokee County assistant manager Maria Hass, County Commissioner Cal Stiles and flight instructor Andy Ernst, Cloer was able to pull off the feat.

"Maria did a lot of organizing work and support for the airport event," Ernst said. "Without her, it might not have worked. It went well, no one was hurt and everyone seemed happy. With that many planes and people walking around with the limited time we prepared, it was really a good event for the county."

Cloer said the airport benefited immensely from the eclipse, selling 1,400 gallons of airplane fuel and 1,000 gallons of jet fuel. The only food vendor who worked at the airport ran out of hot dogs before noon.

Hass said the airport brought in a revenue of around $17,000 during the weekend and day of eclipse, $12,000 of which was earned on Aug. 21.

Four county staff members and their spouses volunteered their assistance during the eclipse event. Cloer said they offered support in parking planes, providing fuel and managing crowds.

"As a team, we were able to get them landed, parked and departed safely," Hass said. "It was a huge success. The event put us on the map. So many people said the town was beautiful, and they definitely want to fly back."

*So many people said the town was beautiful, and they definitely want to fly back.*

People from all over the United States flew in to see the eclipse, including residents of California, Connecticut, Maine, Maryland, New York and Pennsylvania. The furthest plane traveled from Ontario in a bush plane fit for landing in the Canadian wilderness.

Stiles said one of his favorite visitors during the eclipse was a group of skydivers from Greenville, Tenn. The skydivers flew right over the airport and jumped out as soon as the eclipse reached totality.

"It was neat watching because you could look up at the eclipse and see the silhouette of the skydivers," Stiles said.

As soon as totality arrived, Cloer said a peace swept over the airport, halting everything for 2 minutes and 38 seconds.

"It was crazy out here, but once totality hit everyone became silent," Cloer said.

*"It was neat watching because you could look up at the eclipse and see the silhoutte of the skydivers."*

California
Maine Connecticut
Maryland
New York
Ontario, Canada
Pennsylvania
Tennessee

*"Once totality hit everyone became silent"*

# Andrews Middle School raises $40K

Author(s): Kelsey Richardson krichardson@myandrewsjournal.com
Date: August 31, 2017  Section: News (reprinted by permission of The Andrews Journal)

More than 2,000 people gathered at Andrews Middle School during the total solar eclipse on Aug. 21, helping raise about $40,000.
"It exceeded my expectations," Principal Julie Higdon said. "We met so many wonderful people. We were able to network with NASA astronomers, and scientists from all over the world. Some people even came from as far as Israel."
Higdon said all the money raised during the eclipse event will go toward the school's STEM – Science, Technology, Engineering & Mathematics – program. Andrews Middle now has the capability to fund after-school programs and miscellaneous needs students may encounter.

*"Everyone just forgot about everything, and we were all embraced with love,"* she said. *"I cried because we shared this sense of peace."*
Principal Julie Higdon

"The sky's the limit," science teacher Amber Ledford said. "We all agreed as a faculty that we just want to see this benefit our kids by giving them opportunities."

Both Amber and Alaina Ledford, who also teaches science, approached Higdon about holding an eclipse event in January. Higdon enthusiastically agreed, so Amber set off on a planning and public relations quest to put Andrews Middle on the map.

She reached out to NASA, 2017greatamericaneclipse.org, Sky magazine and other astronomy publications. The advertisements drew people from around the world to Andrews Middle, including employees from National Geographic, NASA's Johnson Space Center and the U.S. Forest Service.

She said most serious eclipse viewers set up their telescopes at one of the school's designated fields. Amber said professional and amateur astronomers allowed the public to use their equipment.

"I have been in nerd heaven," Alaina said. "It's probably one of the most eventful times of my life."

Alaina said while she helped with the grunt labor by gridding off fields alongside teacher Ruby Cutshaw, Amber did all of the behind scenes work. Higdon said without the efforts of Andrews Middle staff members and the community, the event would not have been nearly as successful.

In the midst of the event's high-energy atmosphere, Higdon said everyone fell into silence once the eclipse reached totality.

"Everyone just forgot about everything, and we were all embraced with love," she said. "I cried because we shared this sense of peace. Leading up to the event we had been running around, then we just realized how beautiful this work is and how beautiful humanity is."

*"It's probably one of the most eventful times of my life."*
Alaina Ledford

During their stay, the scientists explored the area during the day. They visited Nantahala Lake and could not believe how clear and cold the water was. They drove up Tatham Gap to Joanna Bald to see the views of the valley and received a history lesson on the "Trail of Tears," after returning.

The Andrews Middle School Science Club is to be commended on the organization of such a colossal event. Amber Ledford even took calls on her beach vacation for camp reservations, and all the guests were so pleased with her response time and her knowledge of the event. Not only did they sell campsites, but each one of approximately 500 spaces were marked off and the campers were individually escorted to their campsite by Ruby Cutshaw, Alaina Ledford, Lauren Gentry or Josh Barton.

When the campers pulled in Lenia Yonce, Joselyn Parker-Booth, Sarah Tatham, Lisa Scott and Principal Julie Higdon signed them in. Crystal Jefferies gathered campers together and helped them get on the shuttle. Jenna West, John Worden and Jenny Dalton manned the donut sales and whatever else was needed. There were many staff workers and police officers on call to be of service to the eclipse guests.

In addition to selling campsites, the school sold the campers a meal ticket that was good for breakfast, lunch and dinner. The food was delicious and prepared by Charlene and Dane Rickett. Zack Morgan and Jacob Hogsed manned the bouncy houses and set up the outside movie screen. Avery Cutshaw directed guests and placed many "corn hole" games around the campus for families to enjoy. They also sold T-shirts and donuts as additional fund-raisers. It was the complete package that was excellently executed.

Congratulations to Higdon and her entire faculty for a job well done!

# Edie's Homemade Cookies a Hit in "Totality Town"

Edie Thorpe, who supplies 2 different Farmers Markets with delicious homemade cookies was a vendor at the Andrews, NC celebration.

Andrews earned the name "Totality Town" because it is the only town in North Carolina where the centerline of this Total Eclipse of the Sun passes right through town!

Edie thought it was an amazing and unforgettable experience. And she sold a lot of cookies!

Edie shared, "It was so much fun. I met people from all over the world. A couple from Germany flew over here just to watch the Eclipse in Andrews. Amazing. I had my son and his family here to share the experience. The weather couldn't have been more perfect in Andrews, and when totality happened, everyone was cheering and yelling! It was a great time."

Edie said there were visitors from the following states: New York, New Jersey, Pennsylvania, and Florida, as well as Washington DC. She would like to special order another Total Eclipse of the sun for NEXT summer!

*Amazing!!*

*Unforgettable!*

Munching on Edie Thorpe's homemade cookies, while enjoying the solar eclipse in "Totality Town": Andrews, NC (Cherokee County)

*When totality happened everyone was cheering and yelling.*

**IT WAS SO MUCH FUN!**

Edie took these pictures of the total eclipse of the sun with her Canon Digital camera and a special filter.

*"I wish I could special order another Total Solar Eclipse for next summer!"*
— Edie Thorpe

# STUNNING DIVINE
# EXHILARATING
*Surreal*
## AWE-INSPIRING
### Thrilling
### Memorable
## MAJESTIC
### Exciting
# INCREDIBLE
### POWERFUL
## WONDERFUL
### Joyful
## UNEXPECTED
# Once-in-a-lifetime experience

# Part Four: Gatherings East of the Franklin Area

# Western Carolina University

### First day of classes coincide with the Solar Eclipse!

**All campus was invited to witness Celestial History**

"The celestial bodies are aligning perfectly for the Western Carolina University community to experience a memorable start to the 2017 Fall semester, with the first day of classes coinciding with a once-in-a-lifetime solar eclipse and anticipation rising for all-time records to be set in total enrollment and freshman enrollment."

Quote from: Start of Fall semester – a time to look forward, and up
Randall Holcombe  August 15, 2017

*Classes were canceled from 1:00-3:00 pm*

### 3,500-plus pack Central Plaza to watch 'Great American Eclipse'
BILL STUDENC    AUGUST 21, 2017

More than 3,500 students, faculty, staff and community members packed Western Carolina University's Central Plaza and A.K. Hinds University Center lawn area Monday, Aug. 21, and cast their eyes skyward to get a first-hand look at the Great American Eclipse.

The crowd issued a collective groan as a bank of clouds threatened to obscure the view of the first total solar eclipse in the skies over Cullowhee in more than 500 years, then broke into spontaneous cheers and applause as the clouds parted mere minutes prior to the eclipse reaching totality.

With the eclipse falling on the first day of the fall semester, university officials suspended classes from 1 until 3 p.m. to give students and faculty the opportunity to view the phenomenon. Staff also were allowed to step out of their offices or away from their duty stations to witness celestial history.

WCU Chancellor David O. Belcher said the eclipse-viewing party was a great way to start the year and to build a sense of community around the shared experience as the only University of North Carolina system campus in the path of totality.

"When I first heard that we were going to have a total solar eclipse in Western North Carolina on the first day of a brand new school year, I thought 'really?' As if things are not hectic enough at the opening of a new school year, now we're going to have the first total solar eclipse in this region since the year 1506? And the next total solar eclipse won't be happening for another 136 years? Really?" Belcher said. "But after the initial shock, I realized that this truly is an incredible experience, and that we needed to do whatever we could do to ensure that members of our university community could witness the eclipse," he said.

THE WESTERN CAROLINA UNIVERSITY SECTION IS IN MEMORY OF WCU CHANCELLOR EMERITUS DR. DAVID O. BELCHER

WCU Chancellor David O. Belcher with students during eclipse

The university made available special certified solar viewing glasses so that members of the crowd could watch without risking damage to their eyes by the harmful rays of the sun. The Division of Student Affairs passed out T-shirts and served ice cream, funnel cakes and – of course, MoonPies.

Staff members from the Office of Communications and Public Relations collaborated with colleagues in Information Technology, the College of Fine and Performing Arts, and Campus Activities to mount a 45-minute live online broadcast featuring several subject matter experts and hosted by Brandon Truitt, a 2016 WCU graduate who is now an anchor and reporter at WNCT-TV in Greenville.

In addition to the viewing party in the center of campus, hundreds of eclipse-watchers viewed the eclipse from other vantage points in Cullowhee, including intramural fields, around the Ramsey Regional Activity Center and John W. Bardo Fine and Performing Arts Center and anywhere folks could find a shady spot to set up lawn chairs and blankets.

Head football coach Mark Speir also used the total solar eclipse as an opportunity to debut the black uniforms the Catamounts will be donning for the home opening football game Saturday, Sept. 9, against Davidson, a contest that is being billed as a "black-out game" with fans encouraged to wear black.

## The Old Homestead Tuckasegee, NC

I am blessed to live at the "old home place" in the beautiful Tuckasegee Valley of Jackson County, North Carolina. The little farm is located near the forks of the Tuckasegee River. a m the sixth generation of my Hooper family to call this home.

I, like millions of others, greatly anticipated experiencing the eclipse, particularly because our location was prime for the total eclipse. I wanted to be home with the assortment of "furry and feathered" friends who share their days with me!

We had the usual foggy morning. However, when the sunshine arrived, it was another beautiful day. I prepared an "eclipse luncheon" of fruit and sandwiches, along with a banana pudding (with a moon pie in the center of the topping), Sunmaid raisins, Orbit and Eclipse gum and more Moon Pies. I added small photos of close family members as a tribute to the joy their lives brought to us.

My brother, Denton, and his wife, Alba, joined me. We sat in our lawn chairs, wearing our eclipse glasses. My two hounds, Rocky and Lady, were taking their afternoon naps and slept through the whole event. The roosters and all the hens are free range, so they were scattered all over the field. The guineas, who never cease their communications and security patrols, were everywhere. The Mallard ducks and their babies came from the creek to the yard for an afternoon treat. The four big Welsh ducks (they are like "waddling" pillows) were swimming in their big Industrial-size, aluminum pan.

As we waited and watched, the eclipse was suddenly happening—second by second we could see and sense the rapid changes. It was getting dark and a cloud or two were almost blocking our view, then there was a split-second of the total eclipse! There was not a sound.

As the darkness lifted, I observed the ducks in a "security circle" just as they sleep at night. The roosters all started crowing as if it were daybreak. The guineas began their usual communicating (probably trying to figure out what in the world had happened!) Lady and Rocky finished their naps and came to the porch for a treat. Since today was a very, very special day, they each had a Moon Pie!

It is said that "Our lives are not remembered by days, but by moments" and this eclipse moment is surely a "moment" we will never forget.

*"Our lives are not remembered by days, but by moments, and this eclipse moment is surely a moment we will never forget."*

Firsthand account by:
*Mary Jo (Hooper) Cobb*

# Cowee Bald Fire Tower

My friend Tom Bruce and I hike together a lot, and we had visited the fire tower on Cowee Bald a couple of years ago. When we were trying to figure out where would be a good place to watch the eclipse from, we decided we'd go back to Cowee Bald. We stopped at a grocery store in town to get our tailgate lunch to enjoy before the show. Upon arrival at the top, we discovered that the US Forest Service folks had unlocked and opened the gate, which allowed us access to better parking spots. We broke out our picnic, and dined on the shady side of one of the buildings, as we eagerly awaited the time to move our chairs to the grassy area close to the fire tower.

We were delighted to see that the Forest Service guys had unlocked the top platform of the tower, and we went up to enjoy the 360-degree view, and chat with fellow eclipse viewers. As the time drew closer, we went back down to our chairs and got settled in for the show, ever mindful to keep up with our eclipse viewing glasses.

As the beginning of the eclipse drew near, there were some clouds partially covering the sun, but that allowed us to look directly at the sun without our glasses. The clouds soon moved on, and we were treated to an amazing show. During the time of the total eclipse, everyone and everything got very silent, except for a few oohs and ahs. As the sun came back from behind the moon, there were cheers and applause from the crowd. And as people dispersed and started back to their cars, we were amazed to see the interesting shadows on the ground, as the partially obstructed sun shown through the leaves on the trees. What a spectacular day!

I am already looking forward to the April 8th, 2024, Eclipse, which will probably require a trip to Arkansas to see it!

Firsthand account by:

*Ken Johnson*

# Post Eclipse East Bound Traffic Jam

Less than 1 "eclipse minute" East of Franklin, near Jackson County's Savanah Fire Department on Highway 23, Kyle and Maggie Jennings and their children had a great view of the eclipse. Traffic seemed normal up until the eclipse, but then afterward, for the next couple of hours, eastbound traffic moved at a snail's pace. It was later reported that it took travelers over 3 hours to make the 75 minute trip to Asheville and over 8 hours to complete the normally 3-hour journey to Hickory.

Eastbound

*Traffic moved at a snail's pace*

Looking west there was no traffic.

# Part Five:
# Eclipse Extras

Doug Woodward, Trish Severin, and their family experienced the Total Eclipse while floating in innertubes in the pond on their Thunder Creek property.

# We Survived the Night of Day
## By Rachel Stewart 2017

I woke up to a gorgeous summer morning,
It was just like any other day before.
But this day was unlike any other,
Yes indeed, this day was so much more.
At 2 o clock all was bright and sunny,
But around that point things began to change.
The world outside grew dim and cool,
Crickets began to sing like fools!
Altogether, it felt very strange.

**Chorus:**
We survived the night of day,
We made it through the dark afternoon.
We didn't know what would come
When the sun was blocked by the moon.
For this momentous occasion,
Would our town have enough room?
To house all the extra people
Who came to watch the heavens too?
    But we survived!

For you see this midday darkness wasn't fully "total"
Anywhere that anyone happened to be
But our small town in Western North Carolina
Was within the line of peak totality.
A few months ahead residents began to worry
About how many people would come from out of town
Would roads be overflowed with cars?
Grocery stores laid bare from far
Too many visitors in one locale?

**Repeat Chorus**

Twenty thousand came to Macon County,
We stocked up with things like free glasses for all,
and pulled out our famous Southern charm-based welcomes
For all who drove to heed the heavens' call.
This joyful group stood all as one in shadow,
as moon replaced the sunbeams on the quay
And the great magic of our home,
no longer just for us alone,
brought new friends swearing to return one day..

But we survived the night of day,
We made it through the dark afternoon.
We didn't know what would come
When the sun was blocked by the moon.
With our new friends waving fondly
as they slowly drove away,
We said goodbye to shadow
and enjoyed the sunny day.
We survived!"

Listen at http://m.soundcloud.com/rachels-art/night-of-day

Downtown Franklin, NC Macon County during the eclipse

# Eclipse Song Match-Up Game

Match the Title to the musical Artist then to the Date the song was written

| Title | Artist | Date |
|---|---|---|
| The Dark of the Sun | George Harrison | 1939 |
| Blinded by the Light | Carly Simon | 1991 |
| Ain't No Sunshine | Jimmy Davis & Charles Mitchell | 1973 |
| You're So Vain | Bill Withers | 1976 |
| Eclipse | Tom Petty | 1887 |
| You are my Sunshine | Manfred Mann's Earth Band (Springsteen original) | 1971 |
| Here Comes the Moon | Eliza E. Hewitt | 1979 |
| There is Sunshine in my Soul Today | Pink Floyd | 1972 |

---

The Dark of the Sun- Tom Petty (1991) Blinded by the Light- Manfred Mann's Earth Band (1976) Ain't No Sunshine- Bill Withers (1971) You're So Vain- Carly Simon (1972) Eclipse-Pink Floyd (1973) You are my Sunshine- Jimmie Davis & Charles Mitchell (1939) There is Sunshine in my Soul Today-Eliza E. Hewitt (1887) Here Comes the Moon- George Harrison (1979)

# Eclipse Expressions Word Search

```
C C D D X R Q Z R V G G G T S K T X G R F P E D J
H H Z W B W J R C R N S S O R H P A E N H H C E K
Z E A M A Z I N G I V K U E R A R E D J R X L S I
L E Q T V A E W N O U L H I F M V J A Q C L I O X
E R P C X L A N F R A V L E P B U E U C X C P P E
Q I A E P L U W G T I L P A T S N L L I E G S O R
U N B F M T Y N F J I W K W Z V Q T Z N V F E R U
I G Q R S D B J C N C M H S E H B D B C G L U P T
E P A O H X O T G I S V L Z J N Y S K R T D R L R
T H H H G S U G X F R T N E K Y J X Q E R H W W A
S D S Q Z X X P M K U O I I D Q D E J D E W S Z P
R J H C R I C K E T S D H R F U F G J I N B X W E
S N E K C I H C S P E S G P R J C U D B E C L C D
S U N S E T P O P R D L G R U E I A E L R R A S T
W V I C V C L F A T A G F F R E D X T E E I S T J
C D J F X W I P X S O A K O D A M Q L I S L M A M
C T B D X B E M S Y H K O W Y N Z E C J O A O J E
U U P D M R I E A J C S Z L Z F O K V K H N I U Q
O V N A P B S P M R T I I N I I E M E D C Q A T L
D E D N E P S U S I O M T E M P E R A T U R E L A
F A A Q V D S J N P A N W X E H O J B I W E T M F
T K S K A T S G P F B X A Q G M J J Y B D D Q J I
A H V Y H M Q R X I G Q Y P R X Q F G J A C W X L
S W O D A H S G N I R U C Q H O C W Y N R D P L N
Z E X Z H M S T V S M X A G Q K Z L K M Q V J Q L
```

AMAZING / CHEERING/ CHICKENS/ CRICKETS/ DEPARTURE/ DIAMOND/ ECLIPSE/ EDUCATIONAL/ EUPHORIC/ FAMILY/ GLASSES/ GOD/ INCREDIBLE/ PANORAMIC/ PEACEFUL/ PREPARED/ PROPOSED/QUIET/ RING/ ROOSTING/ SERENE/ SHADOWS/ SOUL/ STIRRED/ STUNNING/ SUNSET/SUSPENDED/ TEMPERATURE/ THRILLING/ TRAVEL

ANSWERS CAN BE FOUND IN THE BACK OF THIS BOOK

### Eclipse: An astronomical haiku

Summer day hangs high
Not knowing a twilight pause
Is a moon away.

Chill of night comes with
A slice of moon seen only
In shadowed pinhole beams.

Sunlight passes on
A three-minute shadow path
Sunday late afternoon
Daytime moon reigns;
Shadows hang like long twilight eves
Slivered sun returns

Birds sing morning hymns
Dawn song brings return of day
Warming beams becon all

White moon overhead
So near the sun- no longer
Will darken daytime sky

## Limerick Match-up

A Limerick is a 5 line poem of a humerous nature.

The first, second, and fifth lines must have seven to ten syllables (same verbal rhythm) with the words at the end of each line rhyming.

The third and fourth lines only have to have five to seven syllables (same verbal rhythm) with the words at the end of each line rhyming.

Limericks are many times written like riddles, that have a kind of twist. The answer may be revealed in the final line.

**IN THE SET OF LIMERICKS, ON THE NEXT PAGE, ABOUT THE TOTAL SOLAR ECLIPSE, YOU SHOULD MATCH UP THE NUMBER NEXT TO THE LIMERICK WITH BEST ANSWER FROM THE FOLLOWING LIST:**

EARTH _____   PATH OF TOTALITY _____
DEFINITION _____   ORBIT _____   SUN _____
CORONA _____ UMBRA _____
ECLIPSE GLASSES _____
MOON _____

ANSWERS CAN BE FOUND IN THE BACK OF THIS BOOK

**1**
A solar and total eclipse
Is like passing celestial ships
As one goes 'front the other
You will soon discover
Night and day momentarily flips.

**2**
Out in space, in a plane, in a tree
Look down and this shadow you'll see
This signature shade
Looks like night when it's made
Lasting minutes— just two— almost three.

**3**
Intersecting celestial paths
Can be calculated with some math
Earth, moon, sun will use gravity
To make circles no cavities
When they cross, it's eclipse aftermath

**4**
This bright burning star heeds the call
When it comes to light and warming all
It's the sol part of solar
And orbit controller
An eclipse will make its daylight fall.

**5**
In a total eclipse of the sun,
The moon separates star from this one
On this planet, moonshade's
Temporarily made
Making lovely, celestial fun.

**6**
An eclipse sees the sun burning bright
Disappear through this small satellite
Our small orbiting friend
Causes tide heights to bend
And can change a bright day into night.

**7**
As the moon passes over the sun
It's not safe to look up at the fun.
Cover eyes with these lenses
And up your defenses
To watch from first shadow to done.

**8**
When planing your day eclipse viewing
there's no reason for sighing and stewing
Many sites map the region
English, Fench or Norwegian
Where the best views will soon be ensuing.

**9**
Eclipses bring dark, 'cept one thing
'round the moon there's a bright golden ring
Though it isn't all sun
It's the light that it's spun
And the sunspots the star just might bring.

Poetry by Debbie Kay

# Eric Haggart
# Professional Photographer

Eric Haggart is a retired US Air Force veteran from the Adirondack Mountains of upstate New York. He and his family moved to Franklin, NC in 2006. Having been on vacation in the area a few years prior, they immediately fell in love with the beauty of the mountains of Western North Carolina and the friendly atmosphere from the residents of the area. His interest in photography grew when he first visited the waterfalls and scenic mountains of the Nantahala National Forest, immersing himself in the technical aspects of photography. His passion for photographing the region led to his photographs being published in many local and regional publications, book covers, magazines, and visitor information guides.

He and his wife, Sonya, love to get out and explore the mountains, waterfalls, and back roads of Franklin and beyond. His latest foray into the photographic and video imaging field has led him to commercial drone operations, creating videos and still photography of the area, as well as real estate, business, and agricultural imaging. His videos and photographs can often be seen in promotion of the Franklin & Nantahala areas on many different social media platforms.

Many of our wonderful photographs in this book are the work of Eric Haggart, including the amazing eclipse photo montage on the Introduction page.

# TOTALITY T-SHIRTS

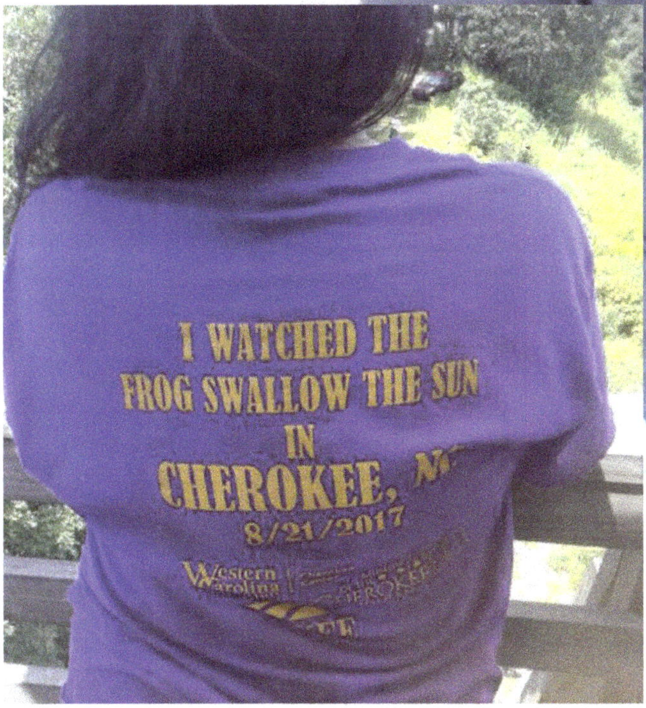

# Shadows
## on Display during the Eclipse

# Acknowledgements

This project has taken the better part of a year to complete. I am grateful for the Town of Franklin, The Franklin Chamber of Commerce, Western Carolina University, Entegra Bank and all of the other eclipse meeting places and individuals for sharing their accounts and stories from the day of the the Great American Eclipse. Several area newspapers allowed us to reprint articles, which helped make this book more interesting.

GreatAmericanEclipse.com gave us permission to use several of their charts and pictures, adding to the depth of this material. Susan Swedlund worked hard on the graphic design and Monica Collier, of Red Press Co., made final preparations for this book to go to the printer. Thank you Doug Woodward for writing the foreword, Rachel Stewart for lending us your song, and John Sill for sharing your beautiful painting of the eclipse. A special thank you to the Suminski Family Books Staff, for the invaluable service you provided on this book.

Deep gratitude to my partner in life and amazing husband, Joe, and our incredible children Annie, Jamy Beth Jerome and Molly, who are my enthusiastic support team for every project. Most of all, thank you to our Heavenly Father for providing this once-in-a-lifetime celestial event.

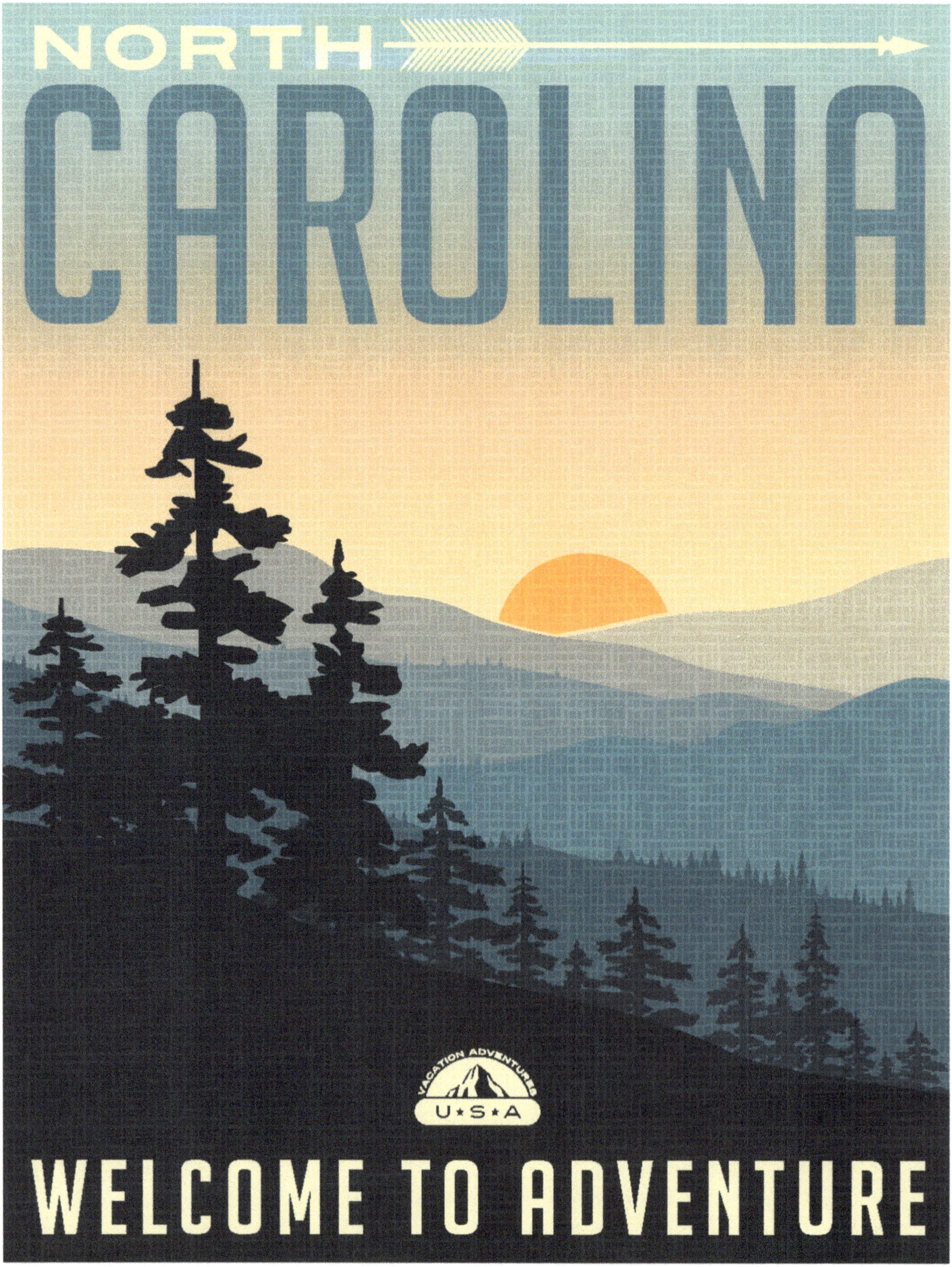
NORTH
CAROLINA
VACATION ADVENTURES
U★S★A
WELCOME TO ADVENTURE

# Meet the Editor: Claire Suminski

Claire Suminski lives in a small mountain community in Western North Carolina. Her husband and four children run a family business and have built a small hobby farm together.

This picture was taken downtown on the day of the eclipse. It was an exciting, joy-filled day that will live long in the hearts of those gathered here to witness and celebrate the Great American Solar Eclipse.
I hope that this record of firsthand accounts will be a great reminder.

*The heavens declare the glory of God; and the firmament sheweth his handywork.*
*Psalm 19:1*

# Meet the Graphic Designer

**Susan Swedlund** is an artist that lives most of the year in Beloit, Wisconsin. Recently she and her husband have been blessed to become part-time residents in Franklin, North Carolina. Susan studied and received her Art degree at Washburn University in Topeka, Kansas. Along with being a Graphic Designer, Susan is a potter and owns the business Potter Sister. While in Franklin, she frequently teaches classes at Cowee Pottery School.

Mosiac pottery piece (5 ft. x 2.5 ft.) done by Susan Swedlund
Visit her website: pottersister55.wix.com/potter-sister to see more of her art work.

# Eclipse Expressions Word Search Answer Key

AMAZING / CHEERING/ CHICKENS/ CRICKETS/ DEPARTURE/ DIAMOND/ ECLIPSE/ EDUCATIONAL/ EUPHORIC/ FAMILY/ GLASSES/ GOD/ INCREDIBLE/ PANORAMIC/ PEACEFUL/ PREPARED/ PROPOSED/ QUIET/ RING/ ROOSTING/ SERENE/ SHADOWS/ SOUL/ STIRRED/ STUNNING/ SUNSET/ SUSPENDED/ TEMPERATURE/ THRILLING/ TRAVEL

# Answers to Limericks:

Earth __5__    Path of totality _8___
Definition __1_   Orbit _3__    Sun _4__
corona _9__
umbra _2__   Eclipse Glasses _7__
Moon _6__

What Fun!

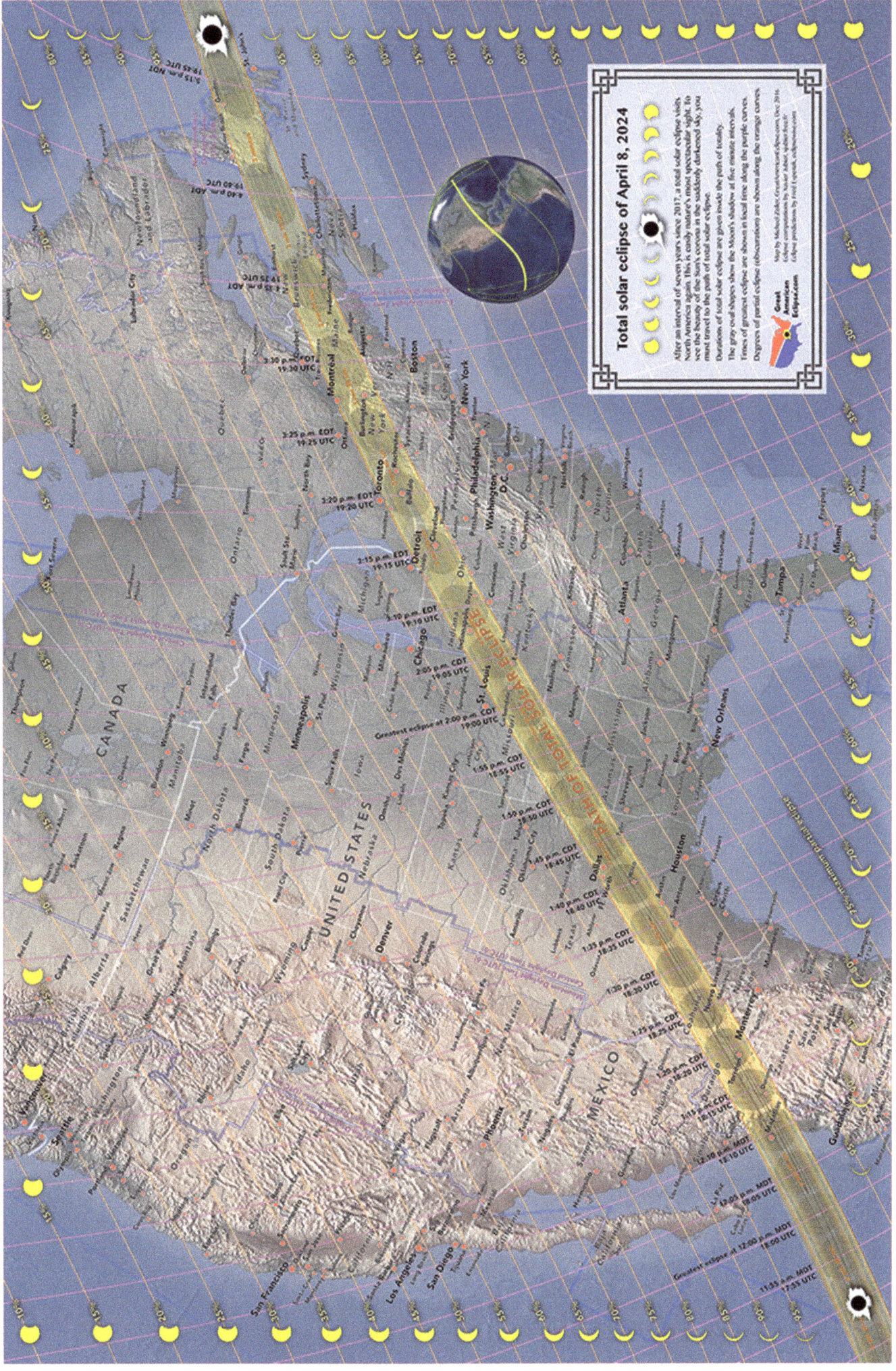

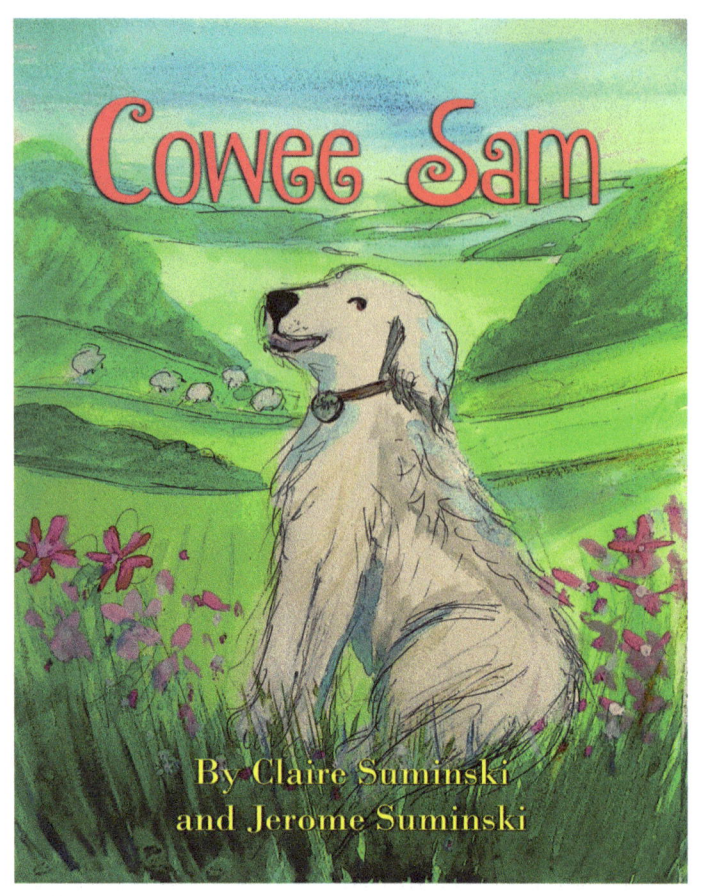
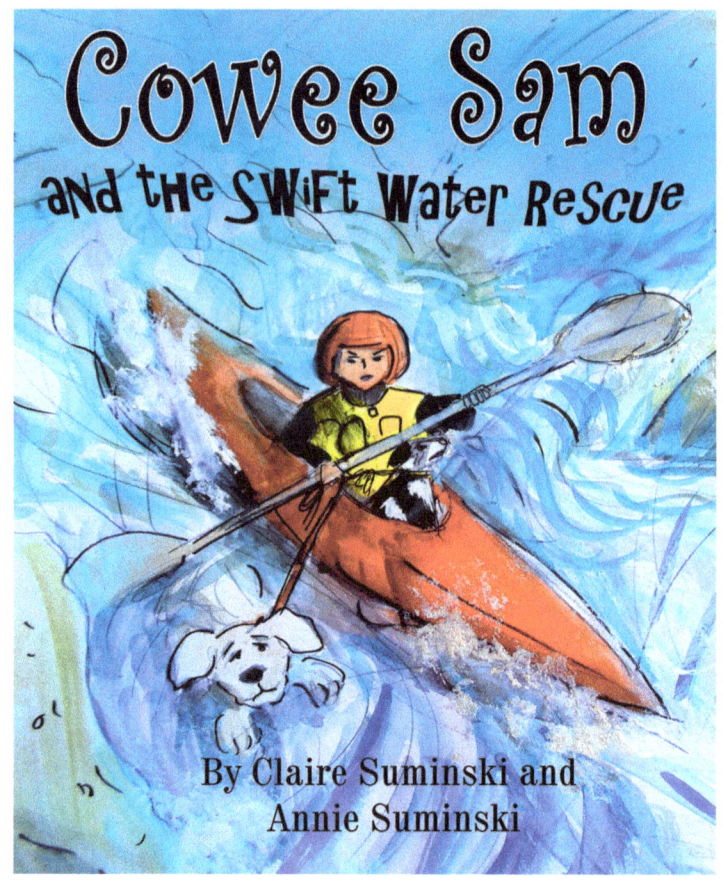
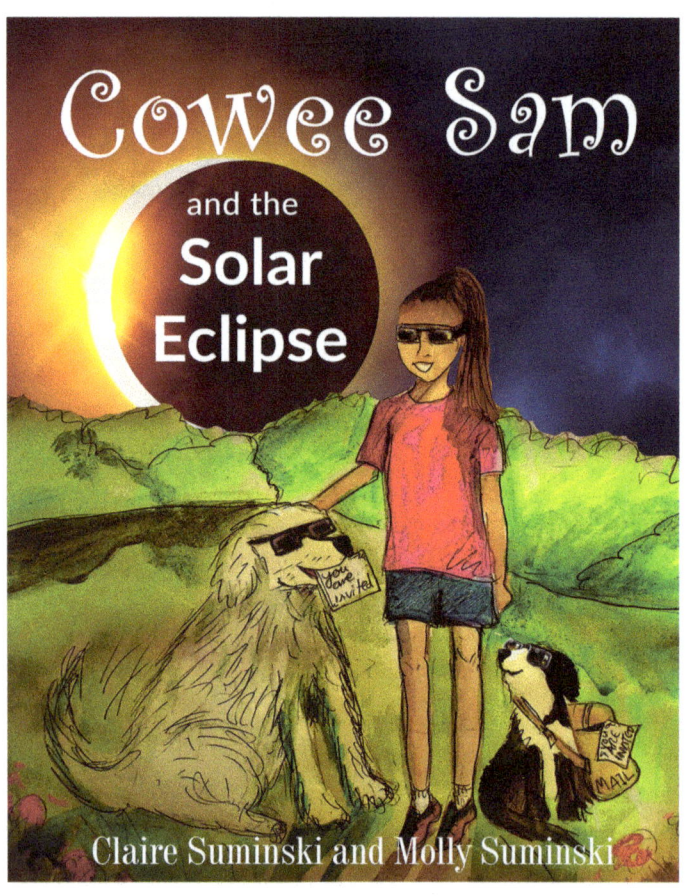

Order more Suminski Family Books on-line at
# www.suminskifamilybooks.com

www.ingramcontent.com/pod-product-compliance
Lightning Source LLC
Chambersburg PA
CBHW040751020526
44118CB00042B/2864